KT-502-625

The Twelve Core Propositions

This book advances twelve core propositions, which are as follows:

I. We all have free will, if we choose to realise it: we do not have to be or remain *victims* throughout life. We can be the artists creating our own lives.

II. We are partly *responsible* for the happiness or unhappiness we experience. We can all make ourselves happier.

III. The still and the harmonious mind is happy and joyful: the unhappy, disturbed, or violent mind is never still. Mindfulness, contemplation, meditation, and prayer are pathways to greater *stillness*.

IV. A life in pursuit of pleasure, e.g. excessive consumption, loveless sex and pornography, is a selfish life. We don't consume pleasure: pleasure consumes us. Happiness is *never selfish*.

V. We all have a *journey* to make in our lives, in search of our meaning or 'song': finding our path, if a humane one, will make us happy. Not finding it makes for an aimless life.

VI. Kindness and *goodness* make us happier: selfishness and unkindness make us unhappy now or in the longer term. It is inevitable.

VII. Bad times and pain are the signals for us to change: however bad and painful life is now, *amelioration* is available.

VIII. Growing old need not be a journey into isolation and loneliness, even with infirmity and loss. *Growing older* can be a path to ever greater wisdom and joy.

IX. Appealing to *higher powers* may assist your journey to meaning and reality. Doing so can help addicts recover. The help is always compassionate, even if the path may be rocky.

X. Probe all your *fixed beliefs*, mindsets, and commitments to ideology, including atheism. Judge less, and be more open-minded and open-hearted.

XI. *Wisdom* and intelligence are different: seek both, but the former more. Education should prioritise wisdom, as high intelligence is no guarantee of it.

XII. Letting go of *attachments* to possessions, thoughts and feelings, especially in the 'second half' of our lives, is the way to the joy and reality that lie beyond happiness.

BEYOND HAPPINESS
ANTHONY SELDON

How to find lasting meaning and joy
in all that you have

yellow
kite

First published in Great Britain in 2015 by Yellow Kite
An imprint of Hodder & Stoughton
An Hachette UK company

First published in paperback in 2016

6

Copyright © Anthony Seldon 2015

Chief Researcher – Adam Davidson

Illustrations by Richard Pope

The right of Anthony Seldon to be identified as the
Author of the Work has been asserted by them in accordance
with the Copyright, Designs and Patents Act 1988.

All rights reserved. No part of this publication may be reproduced,
stored in a retrieval system, or transmitted, in any form or by any
means without the prior written permission of the publisher, nor
be otherwise circulated in any form of binding or cover other
than that in which it is published and without a similar condition
being imposed on the subsequent purchaser.

A CIP catalogue record for this title is
available from the British Library

Paperback ISBN 978 1 473 61944 9
eBook ISBN 978 1 473 61943 2

Typeset by Palimpsest Book Production Ltd, Falkirk, Stirlingshire

Printed and bound by Clays Ltd, St Ives plc

Hodder & Stoughton policy is to use papers that are natural,
renewable and recyclable products and made from wood
grown in sustainable forests. The logging and manufacturing
processes are expected to conform to the environmental
regulations of the country of origin.

Hodder & Stoughton Ltd
Carmelite House
50 Victoria Embankment
London EC4Y 0DZ

www.hodder.co.uk
www.yellowkitebooks.co.uk

For Joanna
who has taken me beyond happiness

Acknowledgements

The author would like to express his gratitude to his principal partners: Adam Davidson, for being a remarkable researcher, and Richard Pope, for all his illustrations. Many of the thoughts and ideas in this book have come from our enlivening discussions. My thanks to Christopher Everett, Anthony Goodenough, Louise James, Tony Morris, Tim Novis, Ruth Scott, Adam Seldon, Joanna Seldon, Jan Stannard, Raine Walker and Simon and Jo Walker for their kind and wise feedback on the manuscript. My colleagues at Wellington College, above all Ian Morris, Delyth Lynch, Guy Williams, Iain Henderson, Robin Dyer, Tom Hicks, Katy Granville-Chapman (the happiest person I know), Angela Reed and Hani Edwards, have been supportive and a source of ideas throughout the evolution of my thinking. I cannot thank enough my partners at Action for Happiness, including Richard Layard, Geoff Mulgan, Vanessa King, Nic Marks, and Mark Williamson. I have learnt much from listening to Adam Seldon, Marty Seligman, Tal Ben-Shahar, James O'Shaughnessy, Robert Easton, James Arthur, Charlotte Style, Peter Read, Jimmy Mulville, David

Yelland, Lil Jones, Caroline Green, Anthony O'Hear, Jane Lunnon and Derren Brown. I owe much to Larry Culliford, author of the insightful *Psychology of Spirituality*. I started writing the book while staying with our friends John and Louise James and finished it staying with Debbie and Felix Francis, who provided a home during Joanna's periods in hospital. Rachel Kelly, author of the stunning *Black Rainbow*, suggested the publisher, readily approved by my agent Ed Victor. Finally, my thanks to the extraordinary Liz Gough, Emily Robertson and all the staff including Veronique Norton and Lauren Whelan at Hodder & Stoughton for all their help and encouragement, and above all, to Helen Coyle for her breathtakingly good and incisive copy editing.

About the Author

Anthony Seldon is one of Britain's most prominent head-teachers and is the acclaimed biographer of several recent Prime Ministers and author of many books on contemporary history and policy. In education, he is most associated with trenchant views on creative learning; bridging the gap between state and independent schools; holistic education and the teaching of happiness, which he introduced at his school, Wellington College, in 2006. In this book, he draws widely on his experience of twenty years as a Head and thirty years in schools, as well as being the father of three children. He has been regularly asked to advise government on education and history, is the founder (with Lord Layard and Geoff Mulgan) of the national body Action for Happiness, launched in April 2011 and is the president of the International Positive Education Network that works to promote positive education for all globally. He became Vice-Chancellor of the University of Buckingham in September 2015.

The Usual Suspects: we all look for happiness in our own ways.

Contents

PART IV — Joy

'Most men lead lives of quiet desperation, and go to their grave with their song still in them.'

Attributed to Henry David Thoreau

PART I

Beyond Happiness

Introduction:
The Imperative to Change

This book is about you finding happiness and joy, but it is also the story of my life. It comes directly out of my experience as a schoolteacher for ten years, a school Head for twenty, a parent to three children, and sixty years of hard and often fraught living. It draws more on my personal experience than the writing of others.

Some years ago, at a difficult point in my life, I was walking along Charing Cross Road in London and stopped to look in the window of a second-hand bookshop. One particular title caught my eye. *How to be Happy.* I stood for a few seconds, gazing at it, and then walked on. But my mind kept returning to that book. A few days later, I went back to buy it. It had gone. This is my attempt to write the book I couldn't find.

I believe there are three distinct levels on which we can lead our lives and that we each have our own intensely personal journey to make through each. This book offers suggestions about how we might move up from one level to another. Reading it should be an active process, one that encourages you to reflect on your own experience. You will almost certainly encounter resistance to yourself. You will discover the role of personal adversity in making that change. Not everyone will choose to progress through the various stages and some people will die remaining on the first level. But this is not inevitable, not for anyone. It is open to every one of us to live a life that takes us beyond pleasure, and beyond mere happiness.

Pleasure	Body	Animal
Happiness	Mind	Human
Joy	Heart	Spirit

The first level of human existence is the pleasure/pain stage, which much resembles the behaviour of animals. Life on this level is dominated by the incessant quest to maximise personal pleasure and to minimise pain. This describes my own life for my first twenty-five years. I was brought up in a privileged middle-class family in the southeast suburbs of London, attending local private schools. I was devoted to my parents but both had had difficult childhoods themselves, and did not find parenting easy. My father was orphaned at the age of three when his mother and father, recent Jewish immigrants from the Ukraine, died in the influenza epidemic that followed the First World War. He was brought up by his Russian stepmother in real poverty in East London. A ferocious high achiever, he rose to head a free-market think tank. I suspect that, subconsciously, much of my inner drive comes from him. My mother's father, a trainee doctor just out of Cambridge, was shot in the head in the First World

War and became an invalid, a writer, a Marxist and a depressive.[1] From her I inherited a profound anxiety.

I was perfectly happy until the age of fourteen when my life suddenly changed, for reasons I still do not fully understand. I found myself prone to all kinds of anxieties, including a fear of going to sleep, and I was plagued by regular depression. My response was hedonism and to take sharp control of my life and the lives of others. I thirsted after pleasure and was blatant in the way that I used people. Confirmation into the Church of England came and went, leaving no lasting impression on me. I flunked my A Level exams badly the first time I sat them (CEE). I was very angry. I organised a mini revolution at my boarding school, Tonbridge, against the school's Combined Cadet Force and the Vietnam War (which ended shortly afterwards), just before my A Levels. I was, generously, allowed back. Just before the new term began, I had experience of deep joy that lasted some days. I returned to school and worked very hard to achieve better A levels. At Oxford I began to direct plays during term time and organise holiday cottages in the long vacations, to ensure that I was always in charge and the centre of attention. I drank every night without exception and smoked heavily. When I was eighteen I had an unfortunate experience with drugs; I feared I had lost my mind. If it hadn't been for that, I might have become a regular user. As it was, I never touched them again.

After university, I knew I wanted to be a writer, a theatre director, a farmer in Wales or a politician (though I could

---

[1] See Robinson, C. (2009). *Arthur Seldon: A Life of Liberty*. Profile Books; Seldon, M. (1985). *Poppies and Roses: A Story of Courage*. Economic and Literary Books; Smith, J. (2014). *Wilfred and Eileen*. Persephone Books.

never decide which party). I became none of these. I opted instead to write a doctorate at the London School of Economics. London was exhilarating in the late 1970s and I soaked up every minute of it until, in my mid-twenties, my life collapsed after repeated failed love affairs. Somewhere inside me I recognised that I could not go on living such a superficial existence, dominated as it was by pleasure and pain.

The second phase of my life began painfully, at the age of twenty-five. It was precipitated by a crisis I suffered when I was in the United States researching and finishing my first book. I woke up in the middle of the night, in the middle of the US, in the middle of a terrifying panic, not knowing who or where I was. Somehow I brought myself back to the UK, helped by Joanna, a new partner who had been a friend since university. With her I began to piece my life together again. I took up meditation and practised yoga twice each day. I stopped drinking and smoking and started to live healthily. After a year or two, I began to feel a lightness and happiness that I had never experienced before. I realised that every decision we take in life makes us either a little bit lighter, or heavier.

I began randomly to fall upon each of the eight paths to happiness that I describe in consecutive chapters of this book, from 'A' for Acceptance to 'H' for Health. I found that happiness is a totally different and much profounder experience than the pleasure I had pursued before. Longer lasting, it emanates from meaningful connection with other people, from harmony with nature and works of art and with the deepest parts of oneself.

For many years following, life was very good. I married Joanna, my saviour and the hero of my life. Building bridges is a deep impulse within me: I had always had a sense that my wife would be black, Muslim, or as in Joanna's case, Jewish. Two daughters and a son came into our lives and I experienced that deep glow of contentment and belonging that parenthood can bring.

Bit by bit, though, from my mid-thirties, the old patterns began to reassert themselves. My career in schools was going well and I became attracted again by glamour and material possessions. Old-fashioned sports cars had always been a weakness, and to Joanna's horror, I purchased several. Finding the time for meditation and yoga became increasingly irksome and they gradually drained out of my life. I started drinking again and returned to the self-absorbed and exploitative behaviour I had known up to the age of twenty-five. Suddenly, at fifty, I found myself in a bleak position. I had become a stranger to myself. I would hear myself talking but it didn't seem like me. I had no peace, either in my mind or out in the world. I was looking for happiness in the wrong places and I fell into a deep depression.

No one noticed any difference initially. I worked even harder at combining being a Head teacher with writing more and more books, none satisfying me. I wanted to be close to my colleagues, but friendships were difficult to find. I began taking Joanna and my children for granted, working excessively, driving myself constantly to the brink of exhaustion. The prospect of living another thirty years seemed very wearisome. Just as everything threatened to overwhelm me, I experienced a moment of epiphany. It was Christmas Eve, 2004. I went to my bedroom, dejected, to meditate. Halfway through, I became aware of a profound inner peace settling in me, and I sensed that everything would be all right. The words of the fourteenth-century mystic, 'All will be well', came to me as embodying a core truth. The experience spoke to me about the inner realm I had lost in my dash for worldly recognition. I gained an understanding that my journey in life was far from complete. Prior to my lapse into discontent I would have said I was happy, but now I realised that happiness could not be the highest state of human existence. I knew I needed to make a fundamental change. But how?

My twin life in schools and as a writer gave me some insights. I noticed that the happiness of children was dependent to a marked degree on the quality of the parenting they received, and that some parents who had great wealth used money as a substitute for love. The happiest and most fulfilled people, and those who had the happiest children, were those who were either not particularly affluent or who had an attitude almost of indifference to their wealth. Both these groups had a sense of perspective about money and recognised that their relationships and their own inner lives were of infinitely greater value. The most anxious and least happy people were those with the most material benefits who lacked any sense of inner value.

At the time of my re-awakening to my own inner life, I was writing a book about Gordon Brown.[2] The experience of writing a series of inside books about Prime Ministers had allowed me to conclude that great power rarely confers happiness. Most of those who've reached the top of politics are anxious and restless. Like Gordon Brown, they are driven by profound unconscious forces to succeed at the highest level, but cannot exist happily when they reach it. It was clearer to me than ever before that there had to be something more to life than money and power.

I began to explore a further five paths, from 'I' for Inquiry to 'M' for Meditation and Mindfulness, this time taking them far

[2] Seldon, A. & Lodge, G. (2011). *Brown at 10*. Biteback Publishing.

more seriously. It was a rocky journey, but increasingly I caught glimpses of a state that took me beyond mere happiness. It could be described as 'joy' or 'bliss', or deepest contentment, but these are only words. The experience felt like being completely loved and accepted, and as if nothing in this world could possibly touch or disturb that state. I was beginning to feel, at last, as if I belonged, that I was coming home.

I recognise this state as the core of my own awareness, as something that is always present, always still and always deeply contented. It exists on a completely different plane to ordinary happiness and can come even in the midst of sorrow and distress. There is nothing self-centred about this experience, which is of goodness, wholeness and completeness. No worldly success or material possessions could hold a candle to this greater prize. The question of how to lead a life that would make this experience the norm rather than a passing rarity became my dominant quest, and I do not imagine that will change until the day I die.

Many sore tests came along the way, none more so than being told in the summer of 2011 that Joanna had an incurable, if treatable, cancer. It has brought us closer together, compelling us to savour the time we spend together and not fritter it away in petty squabbling and trivia. My love for Joanna has deepened immeasurably, as has my love for our children. Grasping that life is finite focuses the mind on what truly matters. There are many challenges and temptations ahead, I know. But I hope I have acquired more wisdom and discernment to guide me than I once had, and a quieter mind.

Ever since my schooldays I have been drawn to trying to help those who are unhappy, but a short time before Joanna became ill, I came across a body of work from the United

States which showed that young people can be 'taught' how to be happier and better able to cope with adversity.

This realisation – that we can *teach* ourselves and others to be happier – was another profound moment in my life. We need not be victims, even if we face adversity in our lives. We can all, with the right information and willpower, improve our lot.

I duly instigated happiness classes at my school, Wellington College. I also decided to begin my weekly staff meetings with a period of stillness or mindfulness. Keen to bring about change on a national level, in 2011 I set up 'Action for Happiness' with co-founders the academic, Richard Layard, and former Downing Street strategy chief, Geoff Mulgan. It is working hard to create a shift in priorities in our culture by helping people take practical action for a happier and more caring society. It provides courses and information and facilitates the setting up of networks to promote happiness, not just in individual lives, but also in homes, schools, workplaces and local communities. It has become fashionable to criticise this approach as most recently in *The Pursuit of Happiness* by Ruth Whippman. Some happiness zealots perhaps deserve criticism; but the core message is sound and good.

This book is aimed at everyone who is discontented with their life, who recognises that it could be much more meaningful and fulfilling but is not sure how to embark on a journey to change. Experience has taught me that life is not random unless we choose to make it so. Adversity need not be negative but may be exactly what we need to encourage us to alter our way of living. Even the most depressed and disturbed people can find solace and comfort and we all can achieve greater levels of happiness. We are never alone unless we think we are or chose to be so. We need to think in a less self-absorbed way and connect more, because ultimately, we are all connected.

This book is not for the faint-hearted. It provides a framework for moving beyond a superficial life dominated by pain and pleasure to one that is suffused with happiness, and then takes us on further to the discovery of joy and peace beyond language. It will take work and dedication on your part, and a willingness to examine your life with a candour that you may not previously have attempted. The book is full of spaces for guided reflection because it is through self-examination that we learn and change. Allowing ourselves as little as ten uninterrupted minutes to explore our feelings and beliefs about a particular aspect of our lives can yield great results. Writing down what comes into our minds is crucial. The act of writing both reveals aspects of a problem we may not have considered and allows us to clarify our feelings. You needn't have any special qualifications to gain from these exercises. Neither do you require any experience of therapy, religious practice, or meditation. All that is called for is a commitment to make time to think honestly about yourself and your actions. You will discover remarkable things, some of which will be painful but many of which will be joyful. Follow this book fully, and you too will discover a sense of coming home.

None of us need to live and die in the pleasure and pain stage. Nor should we stop at the mere happiness level. It is open to each and every person alive, should we will it, to live a life that takes us way beyond happiness. I wish you a fulfilling journey.

Anthony Seldon
August 2014

'I have often said that the sole cause of man's unhappiness is that he does not know how to stay quietly in his room.'

Blaise Pascal, *Pensées*

Pleasure, Happiness, Joy

Most of us profess to love happiness and avidly seek it out. Similarly, most of us hate unhappiness and do everything we can to run from it, to suppress or deny it. Odd, then, that we rarely think deeply about what it is that makes us happy and unhappy, much less examine our role in bringing about those states in our lives. Happiness and unhappiness just seem to happen to us. We either revel in them or suffer from them, helpless and supine. But happiness and unhappiness occur for reasons. This book will explore them. Reading it will allow us to maximise our happiness and minimise our unhappiness. If we want. More than that, it will push us beyond happiness to pursue joy.

This book is full of questions with spaces for you to fill in your responses. Why? Because we mostly read books passively and however much we may agree with them, we are not changed by them. This book seeks to bring about change. It will work if you engage actively with it.

We are all responsible for our lives. Some of us are born with material advantages and opportunities, others with a great propensity towards happiness; some people experience more difficulty in their lives. But we all have free will; we can all make active and deliberate choices about changing the state in which we find ourselves. We just need to begin. The more we exercise choice, the more freedom we have: the less we exercise it, the more we become victims to circumstance.

This book is about the discovery of personal autonomy and freedom. It is about the reclaiming of personal efficacy, about growing in self-awareness and finding ourselves. It is a book that, if you choose, will put you back in the driving seat. Because I believe that, ultimately, none of us truly want to be unhappy. It will take you on a journey in which you will discover profound meaning. Every step of the way will make you feel lighter as you discover your own personal truth in life.

The pursuit of happiness (or joy, as I prefer to term the state of supremely easeful well-being that is this book's aim for your life) is often portrayed as self-centred. Actually, it is anything but selfish. Relatives, friends and colleagues all benefit when we are happy. Their lives are diminished when we are unhappy. The pursuit of joy is a moral duty.

Three states: pleasure, happiness, joy

To understand where we are heading, we need to unpick three quite distinctive states: pleasure, happiness and joy. The attainment of joy is the ultimate end of our lives. The purpose of this book is to help us to arrive at secure happiness, and then to move beyond it.

Pleasure is defined in this book as a subjective state. It is

I. We all have free will, if we choose to realise it: we do not have to be or remain *victims* throughout life. We can be the artists creating our own lives.

transitory and directly experienced through the consumption of material things. It is a purely self-centred, egotistical and narcissistic state. Pleasure is amoral. In experiencing pleasure, we treat others as objects. We are the centre of the universe.

Happiness is a deeper and more rewarding condition. We are no longer isolated individuals but in relationship with others, and with our deeper selves. It is not dependent upon consumption or personal acquisition. We act directly in order to achieve pleasure but we experience happiness as a by-product of living wisely. If we want to be happy, we thus have to live well, and we need to act morally. We must treat others, as well as ourselves, well and justly. To achieve happiness, we need to treat other people as equals.

Joy is deeper still, and is experienced when the profoundest part of us is in complete harmony with the rest of creation. To achieve this state we may need to negate ourselves, our egos, and become one with the whole.

When we experience pleasure, the 'I' is more important than anyone else: we see others as objects. But to achieve happiness, we must treat others as equals. To experience joy, others become more important than ourselves: our whole aim becomes to serve. We can represent this thus.

Pleasure = 1 > 0
Happiness = 1 = 1
Joy = 1 < 0

None of us can move straight to joy. We need first to progress beyond the basic, narcissistic level where our lives are dominated

II. We are partly *responsible* for the happiness
or unhappiness we experience. We can all make
ourselves happier.

by pain avoidance and pleasure maximisation, to experience happiness. When we are happy we mature into rounded human beings, inhabiting a moral world in relationship with each other. Once we have built our secure egos, we have to learn to dissolve them and live from deeper selves, in harmony with the whole of creation. It is then that we experience joy.

Pleasure, happiness and joy, all have their enthusiastic purveyors. Throughout each day, we are bombarded by advertisements telling us that the purchase or experience of this or that product will bring us pleasure.

Some of these pleasures will be harmless but some can damage us and others, when, for example, we indulge in an excess of alcohol, take illegal drugs or have exploitative sex.

Businesses selling transient pleasures succeed because they know that our appetite for pleasure is insatiable. Something about human nature always demands more: bigger, faster, deeper, more intense, stronger, more powerful, more mind-blowing.

The problem is, pleasure derived from a slab of chocolate, or from any other object, always fades when our consumption of it is over. When the sensation dies, the impulse comes into the brain – 'more!' The brain tends to press for still more consumption long after the body is satiated.

The happiness industry, in contrast, sees itself on a more elevated plane. It has ground out self-help manuals for many years, in ever greater volume since the 1990s. Every media outlet dispenses regular advice on how to discover true and authentic happiness. Much of the material is good and based on solid evidence but some is flaky and purely commercial.

III. The still and the harmonious mind is happy and joyful:
the unhappy, disturbed, or violent mind is never still.
Mindfulness, contemplation, meditation, and prayer are
pathways to greater *stillness*.

The study of happiness

The study of happiness has deep historical roots. In ancient Greece, Socrates advocated self-knowledge as the path to happiness. Aristotle believed happiness, or *eudaimonia*, could be attained by living a virtuous life. The ancient Stoics maintained it was achievable via rational thought and an objective perspective on life. They argued that although what happens cannot always be controlled, we can usually determine our response to it. They too advocated a life of virtue to maximise our happiness.

In the eighteenth and nineteenth centuries, philosophers, notably Jeremy Bentham and John Stuart Mill, argued that maximising happiness should be the aim for individuals, for governments and legislators. They gave birth to the term utilitarianism, which advocates the greatest happiness of the greatest number.

In the later twentieth century, the pursuit of happiness was given a major boost by the development of 'positive psychology'. The term was coined by the psychologist Abraham Maslow in the 1950s.[3] Carl Rogers and Erich Fromm built on his work to argue that human beings could work positively and deliberately towards the discovery of their own happiness. But it was not until 1998, when Professor Martin Seligman chose Positive Psychology as the theme for his term as president of the American Psychological Association, that the idea was formally adopted as a discrete branch of psychology.

---

[3] Maslow, A.H. (1954) *Motivation and Personality*. New York: Harper.

Positive psychology claims 'that it makes sense to study what is right about people in addition to what is wrong'.[4] It is concerned with individual lives, as well as with relationships and organisations. The approach is less to analyse and dissect what has gone wrong and to pummel it relentlessly, than to look at the occasions when we ourselves, our relationships and organisations are successful, enjoyable and flourishing. It aims to understand what is happening when things are working well, and to build from there.

Positive psychology has much to commend it. I declare an interest. It certainly inspired me to launch happiness classes in 2006 at Wellington, and to champion 'well-being' and character education at Wellington and beyond. Positive psychology has made a profound difference for the better to many.

Where happiness is limited

End of story? No, for two reasons. Firstly, positive psychology, for all its importance and freshness, works in a morally free or moral-light universe. The happiness described in this book is at heart connected with other human beings and is inextricably bound up with the notion of goodness. Secondly, because even happiness is not enough. It is a necessary but not a sufficient condition for a good life. We are on earth to probe more deeply than that.

---

[4]Seligman, M.E., Steen, T.A., Park, N., & Peterson, C. (2005). Positive psychology progress: empirical validation of interventions. *American Psychologist*, 60(5), 410 at p. 413.

IV. A life in pursuit of pleasure, e.g. excessive consumption,
loveless sex and pornography, is a selfish life. We don't consume
pleasure: pleasure consumes us. Happiness is *never selfish*.

Deep down, somewhere inside us, we *know* that there's more to life than the maximising of our happiness. '[T]here's another country, I've heard of long ago,' is how Cecil Spring Rice described it in the popular hymn 'I Vow to Thee My Country'.[5] This other country, of which we have the most distant awareness, is a land of joy or bliss, imprinted deep in the human psyche. A different kind of business promotes it: the world's religions, in practice often not very well, one has to say. The journey towards joy is from the individual and isolated ego to the fully connected soul. All too often, though, the organisations promoting themselves as religions have become egotistical, serving the needs of those (usually men) who run them, rather than the people who look to them for guidance. Terrible things happen when religions become so egocentric that they claim to have the monopoly on truth, and are entitled to coerce and even kill to enforce that monopoly.

Many religious groups are of course benign; they may indeed take us all the way to the deepest levels of meaning and joy available to humankind, but we must be careful. Whatever their proponents say, religions can only provide the signposts; they are not the destination. Religion as destination quickly becomes a tyranny, and even in the best case, its practice is liable to be superficial if we have failed to realise that we ourselves must be active participants in the search for a good life. I became extremely angry with the concept of religion, and God, when, after I was confirmed at the age

---

[5] The lyrics were set to the music of Jupiter in Holst, G., & Mays, R. (1921). *I Vow To Thee, My Country*. J. Curwen & Sons Limited.

of fifteen into the Church of England, it failed to protect me from life's adversities. Several years were to lapse before my rekindled interest, first in Eastern and then in Western religions, awoke in me the need to take responsibility for my own life and to use religion as a guide on a journey of inner transformation, a journey which is still far from complete.

What then is this destination to which we are headed, this quality or state beyond happiness? Plato provides an important clue in his allegory of the cave in *The Republic*,[6] from the early fourth century BCE. This story is well known. A group of people is imprisoned in a cave for their entire lives, bound so that they can only see a blank wall, upon which their captors are projecting shadows cast by the light of a fire. The prisoners take the shadows to be real. Eventually one prisoner frees himself and turns to look at the fire and the statues used to cast the shadows. He realises he is seeing something more real than what he has always accepted as reality. A greater stage of enlightenment occurs when the prisoner escapes to the world outside the cave and sees trees, animals, the sun. He understands that he is now encountering the source of all light, all life. It is our task as humans to travel outside the cave, to experience reality for ourselves.

Only by finding the depths in our lives and experiencing this reality that lies beyond our subjective minds, do we move beyond mere pleasure and pain. Only in the discovery of joy or bliss can we find true freedom and enduring security. Not as a theory, but as a fact of our lives.

---

[6] Plato (2003). *Plato: The Republic*. Penguin.

V. We all have a *journey* to make in our lives, in search of our meaning or 'song': finding our path, if a humane one, will make us happy. Not finding it makes for an aimless life.

This need to go beyond the individual or self-centred happiness is embedded in the Action for Happiness movement which I helped to set up and launch. In addition to sharing ideas from positive psychology about personal happiness, it encourages members of the movement to pursue a deeper and more altruistic form of fulfilment and to work towards a happier and more caring society. Members pledge to 'create more happiness and less unhappiness in the world around' so this encourages people to look beyond their own happiness and care more for others.

The world's religions preach the 'golden rule' that we should 'do to others as we would have done to ourselves'. I believe this exhortation, to love and to practise compassion, provides the key signpost that we all need. It will take us beyond the pleasures of life, which are often superficial, and beyond happiness, which is a worthy if ultimately limited objective.

What then is this journey, and how might we pursue it? This is the subject of the next chapter.

2.

Life As A Journey

We all choose our lives. Who and what we are today is the result of our past choices. Some of them may not have felt like choices at the time, but they were. We may choose to blame others if we don't like our lives, to blame circumstances or ourselves. But we have always had a choice. An excellent place from which to begin our journey is with the decision not to blame, rather to take responsibility for who we are and resolve to become the person we could be, were perhaps meant to be.

The only inescapable facts of life are birth and death. At any point in our lives we find ourselves somewhere between the beginning and the end. Part of the anxiety but also, if we embrace it, the charm of the game of life is that we never know exactly where we are along that voyage.

Every life, every journey is individual, but they all have something in common. All eight billion people currently on earth have their unique journeys to travel but for all of us, the journeys are in one of two directions: to greater self-absorption and personal aggrandisement, or to greater immersion in compassion and love for others. One direction leads ultimately to fragility, misery and loneliness, which is the state of the individual in isolation from others; the other leads to ever greater and deeper happiness, and to joy.

The epic journey, as in Homer's *Odyssey*, is a common theme in world literature. The hero returns to the point from which he began, having gained in wisdom and self-knowledge. The hero/traveller will have experienced much but is purified by the process and becomes aware of a much deeper self. As T.S. Eliot puts it in the *Four Quartets*, 'And the end of all our exploring / Will be to arrive where we started / And know the place for the first time'.[7]

Along life's way we (in common with the hero/traveller of the epics) experience challenges and tests. They may not be pleasant but they are often precisely what we need, since they offer us the chance to make choices. Without difficulties and challenges, life is not a journey. Without choosing wisely we do not arrive at our desired destination.

It is likely that for much of the time when we are travelling, our eventual destination will be obscure. We may experience it as a 'cloud of unknowing'.[8] It is the direction of travel alone that is important and that direction is always away from self-pity, self-concern and egotism. Deep down, if we allow ourselves space for reflection and candour, we will know whether we are travelling in the right or the wrong direction.

Could it be, in fact, that our lives are 'about' nothing more than this? That the whole *raison d'être* for our birth was this

---

[7] Eliot, T.S. (1979). *Four Quartets* (1944). London and Boston: Faber and Faber.
[8] Originally by an anonymous fourteenth-century writer, see: Walsh, J. (Ed.). (1981). *The Cloud of Unknowing*. Paulist Press.

voyage of discovery, with a divine sense of mystery, or mischief, decreeing that our journey, properly followed, is one that passes from narcissism to self-knowledge, through happiness to joy?

The Journey in Life from Narcissism to Wholeness		
Narcissism / Egotism	Relationship / Maturation	Wholeness / Self-knowledge
PLEASURE	HAPPINESS	JOY

'Most men [i.e. human beings] lead lives of quiet desperation and go to the grave with the song still in them' is a saying attributed to nineteenth-century US poet and mystic Henry David Thoreau, the poignancy of which is not diminished by its uncertain derivation.[9]

We all have our individual 'song', our unique mission or opportunity in life, whether or not we accept it. As we travel on our journey, that inner song is either released, progressively, or it is further imprisoned. When it is fully expressed we at last fully know ourselves, and our purpose. It is joyful. Travelling in the other direction is a journey into obscurity, alienation and misery.

---

[9] In all likelihood this is a combination of misquotation and misattribution. The first part probably comes from Thoreau's *Walden* (1854): 'The mass of men lead lives of quiet desperation'. The second part is probably from another American poem, *The Voiceless*, by Oliver Wendell Holmes (Sr) (1858): 'Alas for those that never sing / But die with all their music in them.'

What is your inner song? Somewhere inside, you may have a sense of it already. On the other hand, you may not have any idea. The work of this book is to uncover it. You can make a start on that process by listing your deepest principles, your values and your biggest inspirations. This is the first box of many in the book which you are invited to fill in. Some may be easier than others. Pass any boxes you do not find straightforward: perhaps you can return to them later.

My principles, values and inspirations

Now that you are thinking deeply about what is most valuable to you, try jotting down any ideas about your life's purpose. We are just setting out on our journey of exploration, so don't worry if you find this difficult. Think back to your childhood dreams. Try to recall any moments, however transitory, when you have been engaged in an activity that is meaningful for you. In the box below, explore your sense of what your life looks and feels like, when you live it well.

My purpose, my mission, my song

Has your vision changed significantly over your life? It's important to understand how it may have become blurred or shifted, and, if so, whether it has done so in a more egotistical and materialist, or a more spiritual way.

In the box above, you started to describe an ideal of your life's mission. Now, in the box overleaf, explore your *current* overriding aim in life. If it is to maximise your income, have more sex or get a new job, then write these goals down. Do not censor yourself.

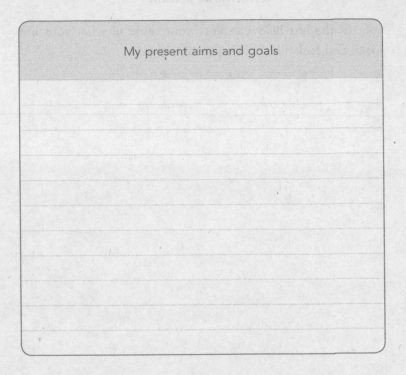

My present aims and goals

Compare what you have written in the two boxes. If they broadly align, your current focus is in tune with your deepest longings and aspirations. If they diverge, as they will for most of us, that is valuable to know, especially if we are prepared to act to align the present reality with our aspirations.

One further thought about how setbacks fit into the pattern of our lives. We tend to see adversity, whether it's the onset of a serious illness, depression, the ending of a relationship or loss of a job, as inevitably unhelpful and to be avoided at all costs. No one can pretend that these incidents are anything other than painful, but along with the pain, they may offer us an opportunity to reassess where we are on our journey. Sometimes difficulties arise because we have fallen off our path or are travelling in the wrong direction. In that case, if we can learn to approach them in a positive and inquiring way, with as much calm and self-knowledge as possible, they may be the prompt we need to get back on the path, or to move along it more quickly. This is one of the most challenging lessons any of us will ever learn: to view adversity as a potential force for good. Don't worry if this idea seems alien to you at the moment. It takes (lifelong) practice to work with this concept. The rewards, though, are immense.

Influences on our journey

None of us is immune to influence, and our choices, and hence our lives, are often composites of the various influences to which we have been exposed. They come in many guises, from the inspirational to the deeply unhelpful. Inspirational people, for example, are vital signposts, though we may not recognise them at the time. Without even knowing it themselves, perhaps, they float for a while into our lives and offer us something profound. We need to be awake or we will not notice them. They can make a profound impression on us if we allow them, because they are talking to us at a deep level. They may be alive or dead, known to us or unknown, real or fictional. People talk to us in many different ways.

List overleaf five such influential figures from the first thirteen years of your life and a further five whom you have encountered since. On the right-hand side, note what it was about them that so inspired you.

Influential figure (from your first thirteen years)	What it was about them that inspired you?
1	
2	
3	
4	
5	

Influential figure (since)	What it was about them that inspired you?
1	
2	
3	
4	
5	

What is it that they have to offer you today? Is there a common thread running through their influences? If so, what is it? What are they saying to you?

As an extension to this exercise, try asking yourself when was the last time you were inspired by someone who has died. The death of a loved one, an acquaintance, or even a celebrity you have admired, can be an occasion to assess how and why they inspired you. Perhaps you have been to a funeral or memorial service or read an obituary that particularly inspired, uplifted, or made you think profoundly? Now close your eyes and imagine your own funeral or memorial service. What would you like to hear said about you? What are the values or traits that you would like to have attributed to you? What are the differences that you have made to people or groups? What achievements and successes?

You might find this exercise macabre; you might be wondering what it has to do with happiness. Everything. Happiness and joy arise from a journey well travelled; unhappiness and confusion from a journey not travelled, or not travelled well. There is nothing tougher than to contemplate death, our own or that of the people we love and admire, but it can be the key to kickstarting our journey towards a more meaningful life.

People are not the only influences in our lives. Make a note now over the page of any books, films or stories that have helped you understand the direction you should be travelling. A core story for me, which I came across in my twenties and which resonates just as strongly with me today, is as follows.

'The Grand Rabbi of Lyons was a Jewish chaplain to the French forces in the 1914–1918 war. One day a wounded man staggered into a trench and told the Rabbi that a Roman Catholic was on the point of death in no-man's-land, and was begging that his padre should come to him with a crucifix. The padre could not quickly be found. The Jew rapidly improvised a cross, ran out with it into no-man's-land, and was seen to hold it before the dying man's eyes. He was almost immediately shot by a sniper; the bodies of the Catholic and the Jew were found together.'[10]

The stories that most inspire you

[10]Gollancz, V. (Ed.). (1955). A *Year of Grace: Passages Chosen and Arranged to Express a Mood about God and Man (Vol. 1091)*. Middlesex Penguin Books.

Neither all the influential stories nor all the significant people you have encountered will have been productive or rewarding. Some of them may have damaged you or otherwise cast you off your path. Our journey is hazardous and full of encounters that are unhelpful, and of people who purport to have our best interests at heart but who don't. We have to learn to discriminate the good from the bad.[11]

In the box below, list some of these people, events or stories that have damaged you, led you to beliefs that were unhealthy or in other ways thrown you off what you suspect may be your true path. You may have to probe hard to identify them and it can be uncomfortable to be this candid, but it is important to try. An example from my own life: I remember feeling that, after graduation, I had to match university friends in terms of status, power and possessions. We had been equals in college and it was disconcerting to see our paths diverge. I felt insecure and inferior by comparison. These feelings led to some very superficial choices on my part.

> ### Influences that have taken us away from our journey

---

[11] The book of Genesis, chapter 32, provides an illustration of the difficulty of understanding whether someone is friend or foe. In the story of Jacob's encounter with the angel at the ford of Jabbok, it is not clear whether the one he wrestles with is for him or against him. With thanks to Ruth Scott for this example.

·The company we keep is of considerable importance. Very few people are strong enough to rise above the dominant group or groups with which they associate. Our attitudes, preferences, beliefs and actions are powerfully conditioned (to an extent that we may not like to acknowledge) by the company we keep.

Be honest about the group or groups to which you belong. Do they uplift and inspire you? Do they make you feel good about yourself? Or is their overall approach negative and destabilising? If it is, what are you going to do about it?

Buddhists have a term, sangha, to describe the association or company of like-minded people in pursuit of greater understanding of the truth. Such communities are found among all religions and among the non-religious. They can be powerfully supportive in helping us achieve our desired direction of travel.

The most significant ally or enemy we will encounter on our journey is ourself. If this is a journey into self-discovery, we have to get to know ourselves profoundly: our feelings and thoughts, our fears and desires. There will be much that we do not like about ourselves. The way to be free is to see what is inside us and choose to accept it with equanimity. Do not follow negative thoughts such as, 'I cannot do this. I cannot make this journey' or 'I am not good enough'.

Hiding from our journey

If we choose not to leave our front door and to venture out into the great unknown, we lose our ability to discover depth in our lives. Tomorrow will be like today, because today was like yesterday. The only change some of us ever experience is our demise. In the end, the journey of life is the inescapable reality for us all. We may blunt our awareness of it with self-delusion, with constant busyness, with chasing after success, the thrill of acquisition or with alcohol and drugs. But we cannot hide forever: sooner or later we have to be counted. We have to take responsibility for our lives. Denying the existence of our personal journey does not make it disappear. We will all die. We will all have funerals of some sort. Shakespeare pinpointed the transitory nature of our brief time on earth when he wrote, 'I wasted time, and now doth time waste me'.[12] The sooner we start to acknowledge that we have a journey to make, the better. It will take us from pain, beyond happiness, to bliss.

---

[12]Shakespeare, W. (1935). *King Richard II*. Chiswick Press. Act V: Scene 5.

Of course, the impulse to hide is understandable: most of us fear death. Whether or not any part of our being continues after death, those who have lived lives full of love face the prospect of their demise with much greater peace. It is natural to worry about those we love, left behind, natural to mourn our loss of them and theirs of us, but we should try not to be transfixed by it. I suspect that death itself may not be the problem. Rather, a life not well lived could be the source of our ultimate anguish. If we have led a bad life we will be afraid of death, and with reason: not because of any torments in an afterlife, but because of the terrible waste of our time here. But if we have led a life full of compassion and goodness there is nothing to fear or to rage against as the darkness approaches. Instead of quivering in fear or rage, get on your path. I promise you it is never too late.

This is why I'm very proud that our Action for Happiness movement is all about helping people to go beyond self-centred happiness and to focus on living in a more compassionate and loving way. The movement is building very strong support (including from the Dalai Lama, who is now its patron) and thousands of Action for Happiness supporters are joining together to share this more authentic and lasting form of happiness and to promote a more caring and altruistic culture.

Pain, Unhappiness, Hell

Pain, unhappiness and even periods of acute misery that could be described as hellish, are experienced by most of us as part of our human existence. Some of us have only a transitory encounter with them while others, often for no apparent reason, find their lives immersed in them.

We need to understand all three terms, and to see them as the flip sides of pleasure, happiness and joy. Pain may be unavoidable in many circumstances but is often the misuse of pleasure; unhappiness is caused by living unwisely and by attachment to happiness, while hell is alienation from our source of joy.

Pain

Pain is a constant of the human experience. We suffer in our bodies, our hearts, our minds and even, I would argue, our souls. My focus here is on the pains of the body; those of the mind and soul I term 'unhappiness' and 'hell' respectively.

VI. Kindness and *goodness* make us happier: selfishness
and unkindness make us unhappy now or in the longer
term. It is inevitable.

Some of the physical pain we suffer is the result of not looking after our bodies properly. Back pain can result from poor posture and dental pain is exacerbated by lack of care in looking after our teeth. Soft tissue damage can occur when we exercise to excess or have accidents playing sports, often when the body is out of shape or not warmed up properly.

Pain can equally be brought on ourselves by unwise living. Eating too much, or the wrong kinds of food, or having insufficient hydration, can lead to pain in the body as well as to low energy and self-esteem.

Excess alcohol leads to hangovers and other maladies in the short term and to liver disease, cancer and misery in the long term. Recreational drugs might deliver a hit of pleasure but pain and agony follow eventually. Smoking can be enjoyable for those first few seconds of inhalation but will almost certainly bring disease and suffering in the end. We know this, of course, and yet many of us continue. It takes practice to be able to refocus on the long-term perspective. Human beings are not very good at it and willpower is a notoriously limited resource. The work of this book will help to shift your focus so that it gets easier.

Unhappiness

Unhappiness can be caused by many things, but I want to suggest that a primary cause is a counter-intuitive one: the attachment to happiness. Happiness is of course a desirable thing, and it is certainly more rewarding to have a life full of happiness than one that is dependent upon mere pleasures.

Being happy, and being around those who are happy, is fulfilling and uplifting. But the pursuit of personal happiness, despite what utilitarians, positive psychologists and other happiness ideologues have argued, can never and should never be enough for any human being. Such happiness can all too easily be narcissistic. At the heart of happiness, as positive psychology describes it, is an emptiness, an unanswered question and a self-centred existence. There remains a sense, however remote, that there must be more to life.

The problem with making happiness, in this sense, the goal of our lives is that the potential for unhappiness is ever present. Such happiness is always reliant upon a person, a mental state or a physical object for its fulfilment and meaning so it is always contingent, never immutable.

Martin Seligman, the lead figure in positive psychology, spent many years puzzling out how to help others find happiness before alighting on an answer. It can be summed up in the acronym, 'PERMA', where the five letters stand for Positive Emotions, Engagement, Relationships, Meaning and Accomplishment.[13] Embrace each, and happiness, he says, will follow. Grounded in years of research by psychologists, this approach provides valuable strategies for achieving happiness and reducing unhappiness. It has made a major contribution to the alleviation of depression and the achievement by many of more fulfilling lives. But each of Seligman's five approaches has its limitations.

A focus on 'positive emotions' as opposed to dwelling on

---

[13] Seligman, M.E. (2012). *Flourish: A Visionary New Understanding of Happiness and Well-Being.* Simon and Schuster.

negative feelings allows us to feel and perform better, and to raise the spirits of those around us. But ultimately we are being asked to aspire to an emotional state which may sometimes be beyond our powers, and which may also be dependent upon factors largely outside our control.

'Engagement' exhorts us to become absorbed in what we do, thereby attaining a state that positive psychologists relish, called 'flow'.[14] We achieve this by acting from our strengths (a core term in positive psychology) and by absorbing ourselves in activities that we love. This emphasis on engagement, however, has limitations because where it is not attained, perhaps through no fault of our own but simply because we are not fired up by what we're doing, there will be unhappiness. We must seek something beyond engagement on which to depend.

'Relationships' are clearly fundamental because humans are social beings, and our happiness is immeasurably enhanced if we have supportive and loving relations with family, friends, colleagues and neighbours. Happiness is magnified when we share our happiness with them. Basing our happiness upon relationships, however, is always precarious. Families can be as much a cause of grief as happiness, colleagues can turn against us, friends or loved ones can disappoint or abandon us, or die. Relationships are always contingent; we can never, should never, depend upon them entirely for our happiness.

'Meaning' is essential for happiness because life without it

---

[14] The concept of 'flow' is associated with the work of celebrated psychologist Mihaly Csikszentmihalyi, see: Csikszentmihalyi, M. (1991). *Flow: The Psychology of Optimal Experience.* New York: Harper Perennial.

is aimless. The problem with 'meaning' is not that the aim is unworthy, but that, as envisioned by positive psychology, it does not take us as far as we should be aspiring. Positive psychology is concerned with finding 'a' meaning, rather than 'the' meaning, for our lives.

'Accomplishment', finally, suggests that happiness is found with the achievement of our personal goals. There is much truth in this. But basing our happiness upon accomplishment is always a risk, because it is always conditional. Many high achievers are chronically dissatisfied. Our accomplishments can always be denigrated by others. They can be taken away from us. Pin too much of our fulfilment on accomplishments and we tread on thin ice.

Unhappiness, or depression, does not appear to be reducing with greater material affluence and developments in medical and psychiatric treatment. More troubling than the flip side of pleasure, i.e. pain, unhappiness seems to strike many of its victims wantonly. We need to probe unhappiness and its causes further, and to explore how we can choose to be happy. Perhaps it would be helpful to remember the Jewish wedding tradition of breaking a glass just after the groom has given his bride her ring. We should never forget that unhappiness can be present even in the midst of great happiness.

Hell

Still more painful than unhappiness is the hell we experience if we lose our way in life and find that we cannot return to the path we once walked. Hell is the flip side of joy.

We can experience hell if we knowingly knock others off their path, or damage their happiness. Why is it that people who are genuinely kind and compassionate are much happier than others? Why are unpleasant and selfish people so often miserable? And seriously unpleasant people become, sooner or later, seriously miserable?

Karma, a key concept in Hinduism, Buddhism and some other religions, states that our actions and intentions will affect our future. Good actions will bring us happiness. Bad deeds and intents will bring us suffering. The law is inescapable; being ignorant of it does not exempt us from its hold over our lives. This can feel like a challenging idea but it is not dissimilar to the Judeo-Christian concept of doing unto others as we would be done by, which finds cultural expression in Dickens' Scrooge in *A Christmas Carol*, for example, who finds joy only when he recognises the injustice of his treatment of others. Ask yourself whether some of your suffering has been brought upon you in this way. I have noticed that when I treat others badly I go through a three-phase cycle in response: internal attempts at self-justification; a realisation that I was unjust; a searching for the right way to make amends.

Some suffering feels inexplicable and devastating – a terminal illness, a serious reversal or a tragic accident, for example. But even when it appears capricious or unjust, we still have the freedom to respond in ways that will suffocate or free us. Terrible things happen but how we react to them makes their effects either greater, or lesser. Summoning our reserves of compassion, for others and ourselves, is a difficult but highly effective way to struggle above the hell of suffering.

The intense experience of hell is almost impossible to

describe but words like 'unrelieved misery' and 'agony' give a glimpse into its depth. Those who have never experienced it can struggle to understand how dreadful it is. Those who have experienced it find it hard to talk about. The state is real, though. Hell may or may not exist after life. It most definitely exists on earth.

PART II

Pleasure

'If only we'd stop trying to be happy, we could have a pretty good time'

attributed to Edith Wharton[15]

---

[15] In fact the quotation is 'If you make up your mind not to be happy, there's no reason why you shouldn't have a fairly good time' – from *The Last Asset* (1904), in Wharton, E. (1989) *The Collected Short Stories*. R.W.B. Lewis (Ed.). Scribner.

Benign Pleasure

The maximising of pleasure and the minimising of pain, as Freud said,[16] is a good description of the aim of many people's lives. But to imagine that this is all they can or should amount to, would leave us little better off than animals. As John Stuart Mill wrote, 'It is better to be a human being dissatisfied than a pig satisfied; better to be Socrates dissatisfied than a fool satisfied. And if the fool, or the pig, are of a different opinion, it is because they only know their own side of the question.'[17]

Animals, like babies, demand instant gratification. They lack the will to delay eating and other pleasures, to understand that pain might sometimes be necessary, and that there are higher ends in life than the chemical sensations in the brain that pleasure and pain induce.

Not that pleasure is in itself the problem; in fact, pleasure is

---

[16]Freud, S., Bonaparte, M.E., Freud, A.E., Kris, E.E., Mosbacher, E.T., & Strachey, J.T. (1954). *Project For A Scientific Psychology.*

[17]Mill, J.S. (2007). *Utilitarianism, Liberty & Representative Government.* Wildside Press LLC.

one of the great gifts of life. Individuals and societies that frown upon it suppress their own capacity for enjoyment as well as trying to deny it to others. It is a misunderstanding of religion, made by Puritans and some fundamentalists, to believe that pleasure and enjoyment are evil, and that denial of them is necessary for achieving higher spiritual levels. It is only when pleasure becomes our principal goal that it goes wrong. Similarly, we go awry if we become overly obsessed with avoiding pain, some of which will be inevitable and indeed useful.

How far is your life dictated by the maximisation of pleasure and the minimisation of pain? List below your five principal pleasures and the five sources of pain that you are keenest to avoid.

	Principal pleasures	Main sources of pain
1		
2		
3		
4		
5		

Some people deny themselves pleasure as a form of self-punishment. In fact, benign pleasures add greatly to our motivation, and our determination to achieve. They come in many forms, amongst them bodily, possessing, recreational and aesthetic pleasures.

Bodily pleasures

Most of us take our bodies for granted. We do not think that they require conscious awareness, so we let a whole gamut of bodily functions take place without awareness of what is happening, or conscious decision on our part. When we allow our minds to run on autopilot, we are not fully human, and we also miss out on pleasure. Most bodily functions can be a source of pleasure eventually, if we are mindful of what is happening.

Breathing, for example, is an automatic bodily response, though we have the important freedom to slow down or speed up our rate. If we sit still and are conscious of the breath coming in and out of the body, and the lungs rising and falling, we will derive pleasure just from noticing what is happening.

Daily meals are consumed with little awareness of what we are eating: the tastes, the flavours, the textures, the combinations, even the colour: all are taken for granted. When you consume your next meal, decide to taste every mouthful. Notice the touch of your hands on the cutlery and the flavour of the food and drink in the mouth. Notice the different aromas. Doing so is a completely transformative experience. Our pleasure in our food will mount the more aware we are. And we do not have to go out to an expensive restaurant to increase our enjoyment of food. We may indeed pay vast amounts to eat out and consume expensive wine, without ever really engaging our taste buds.

In the same vein, we can walk from A to B but often our

body walks without our minds consciously being aware of our journey. Try being more observant of your surroundings and notice the difference. Derive the pleasure that is there for the taking by noticing the wind passing over your face, the sights, the sounds, the slap, slap, slap of your feet on the ground. Better still, when conditions permit, walk barefoot, which, for me, is one of the greatest pleasures known to human beings.

It wouldn't be a good idea to advocate smoking but as a regular smoker, many years ago, it turned out to be an aid to awareness. I noticed that I was only conscious of one inhalation in maybe a hundred cigarettes. When I was consciously aware of exhaling, then there was pleasure. This helped me to recognise how often the mind is absent. Savouring wood smoke from an open fire can provide similar deep satisfaction. Perhaps smoking is satisfying because it is a connection with earlier ages when human beings lived closer to nature. Similarly, pleasure can be derived from listening to running water or smelling fresh baked bread.

With sex, the desire for the orgasmic gratification all too readily trumps the pleasure of the journey. And sleep is perhaps the greatest pleasure of all. Let the mind be present in the body, not agitated about the day that has just gone or the day to come, but fully tuned in to the quiet, comfort and security of your own bed.

Possessing

The pleasure of possession can perhaps be explained by the boost it gives our sense of security, as well as the desire to flaunt our purchasing power. There is also a pleasure to be derived from collecting things that intrigue or interest us, and they don't have to be particularly valuable. As eBay testifies, there is barely an object that cannot be collected and enjoyed. Even the youngest children become very attached to their favoured objects and in fact these early attachments can endure through life, as the widespread presence of teddy bears in adult beds confirms. The possessions we often are most reluctant to part with are those that date back to our earliest years, which we associate with the happiness and security of childhood.

A particularly healthy way to enjoy the pleasure of possession is perhaps to derive joy from those things that are in any case a necessity, such as clothes. Dressing well, in a manner that expresses our personality and taste, will enhance our enjoyment of daily life.

The degree of pleasure we can derive from the homes we inhabit bears little relationship to their relative poverty or grandeur. Attitude is all. Some of us find it hard to accept our homes as they are; we would prefer them altered, bigger or better. Our pleasure is diminished because we compare our homes and our possessions unfavourably to those of others.

Possessing our own means of transport has been a source of satisfaction throughout history. It becomes an extension of personality. An animal, a bicycle, a motorbike, or car, provide exquisite pleasure: the thrill of looking, touching and even smelling it, the joy of its motion, the beauty in form and substance.

I would argue that the pleasure derived from having a pet or merely being in the presence of animals, can be intense. Sometimes it seems to me so profound that I wonder whether our lives can be appreciated to the full without this deep, even mystical boon.

Recreation

Derived from the notion of re-creating or renewing ourselves, the very word 'recreation' suggests that a life spent only at work and taking care of the essentials of food, shelter and clothing, is incomplete. And so it is. No recreation, no regeneration. Just entropy.

Most of us give too little time to recreation. We work hard, play light. We assume that play is the entitlement of every child, even if opportunities for many children to play outside are diminished by the restrictions of urban life. Many of us think we are too busy for hobbies or that play is frivolous, not a good use of our time. The truth is, recreation provides vital pleasure, a creative outlet and energy- and mood-boosting fun for all, regardless of age or circumstance.

Note below any recreations you once enjoyed for which you no longer find time, or any you think you might like to take up.

Desired or under-realised recreations
1
2
3
4
5

Recreations vary from the immobile to the highly active, and from the mentally inert to the highly taxing. Many of us claim that we want to relax more but in fact, relaxing can be one of the most demanding of recreations, because it requires a positive decision to sacrifice activity and to let go, whether stretched out on a beach under the sun or propped up on a settee at home. Learning to relax, without shame, without guilt, is one of the great arts and solaces of life.

Reading is another pleasure that requires willpower if we are to incorporate it into our busy lives. Setting a target of reading, say, a book a month, is good discipline. What you read is of course up to you but it needn't be self-consciously worthy material. Some people feel they have to keep up with the latest novels, while others make themselves read the classics when they would rather be reading thrillers. Such attitudes contribute to the way that the exquisite pleasure many of us experienced when reading as a child, perhaps in bed, can all too easily be lost in adulthood. For me, the intense solitude of reading is one of its attractions but we do not have to read alone. Book groups, poetry and play reading societies all provide great enjoyment, as their continuing popularity shows, as well as much happiness from the shared experience.

Hobbies such as fishing, bird watching or trekking were often passed from parents to children. Opportunities for children to embrace nature have declined: what will take their place?

Children equally benefit from early exposure to the arts, at home and at school. Governments are wrong not to be doing more to introduce young people to art and culture via their education. The children who suffer most are those from backgrounds where they are unlikely to encounter literature, music, theatre or visual arts at home. Some people feel that such things are not for them, that it is all too high-brow, too complacent or self-obsessed. But there is something for everyone, whatever their taste. Playing a musical instrument and singing, painting and drawing, looking at art and architecture, writing creatively, dancing (whether it's ballet or ballroom) and watching dance, participating in and seeing drama all impart great pleasure. So too does supporting sports teams, from watching them to immersing ourselves in the lore of the club or team.

High-street shopping, a great British pastime, is under threat from the perceived convenience of impersonal out-of-town stores and on-line shopping. Local economies need local shops. The pleasure that comes from using them and seeing them flourish is very rewarding since it feeds our need to belong to a community.

Exploring and travelling are pleasures that enrich our lives, especially when we have time to immerse ourselves in the local culture, cooking, peoples and traditions. The pleasure is diminished if we hide behind an iPad or mobile phone screen, using photography as a substitute for direct experience.

Aesthetic pleasure

Recognising and appreciating beauty provides one of the profoundest pleasures in life.

The beauty of the natural landscape can be much enhanced by experiencing it on foot, bicycle, boat or riding through it on an animal. Present-mindedness enhances immeasurably our pleasure from natural beauty by bringing us into the moment. Allowing ourselves to be still by a river or on the shore of the sea lures us away from our mental abstractions into the reality of nature itself.

Education is required if the built environment is to be fully appreciated. Schools should teach architectural and engineering history, to allow students to appreciate the beauty of cathedrals, bridges and modern towers. We need to look up from the shop windows to the architecture above if we want to appreciate the full beauty of our towns and cities. The shops might have names common across the world but the buildings in which they are housed are unique and each has their own history and aesthetic.

There is no shame in admiring and taking pleasure in the beauty of the human form. Artists throughout history have responded to this fascination. Their desire to represent it mirrors our need and pleasure in looking. Becoming obsessed by beauty, though, and indeed becoming obsessed by any of our pleasures, takes us beyond a tipping point to where pleasure turns negative, as we explore in the next chapter.

Harmful Pleasure

Pleasure and pain are much closer than we care to think. Our experience of both places ourselves at the centre of the universe. As we have seen, a life that is merely lived in pursuit of the maximisation of pleasure will be a superficial one, with pain the inevitable result.

Bodily pleasure and pain

Physical pain is the most common form we experience. If we misuse our body, by exercising it excessively and straining it, or exercising too little, then pain will result. Eating badly or to excess will also cause pain.

Alcohol is one of life's greatest pleasures, from its subtle tastes and aromas to the mental states it induces. But in excess it damages us and others. Drug takers and excessive drinkers are sad partly because they are so boring. There is little sharing. It is a masturbatory exercise dressed up as social engagement.

Sex can provide great and exquisite pleasure and, in a

VII. Bad times and pain are the signals for us to change:
however bad and painful life is now, *amelioration* is available.

respectful relationship, will bring happiness as well. The respect extends to our partners. Infidelity may give us short-term pleasure and excitement but will generally lead to pain and remorse, which will ripple ever outwards. When sex is merely for the gratification of our needs, it will eventually result in pain to others and ourselves. Sex is one of life's metaphorical explosives and needs far more care than many people deploy.

Pornography is a classic example of a harmful pleasure since it is always based upon exploitation of others. You will not see many happy faces or eyes in those providing our titillation. Pornography is rooted in the objectivisation of other human beings. We have no relationship with these people, they are no more than objects of gratification to us. After the pornography exposure is over we feel cheap, not uplifted. We have dehumanised ourselves, and the more pornography we consume, the more dehumanised we become.

Fifty Shades of Grey has sold over 100 million copies. It may have released unhelpful inhibition and given widespread pleasure. But how many have been made happier by reading the book or seeing the film? Has it loosened martial bonds as it is tightening sadomasochistic ones, and resulted in emotional as well as sexual pain, and made many feel inadequate?

Our bodies are a gift. We rely on them absolutely yet none of us is handed an owner's manual that explains how we should use them to best effect. Painful mistakes are often necessary to help us learn.

Possessing as an end in itself

Ownership goes awry if it becomes too important to us. We can never truly 'possess' anything or anyone. We might have purchased an item, have a legal title to a property or enter into a marriage contract with another but we are only ever the temporary and partial possessors. Legal ownership is always paper thick. The Egyptian pharaohs were among the powerful and deluded who tried to take their possessions into their next life. We laugh at that, but we fail to see that we try to do the same.

Making our possessions an end in themselves is a formula for pain. Our goods will decay, they will be sneered at by others, their value is volatile and uncertain, they can be stolen and always run the risk of being lost.

Trying to 'possess' another human being, as many lovers and many parents try to do, is even more crass. Kahlil Gibran, the author of *The Prophet*, summed up the parochial fallacy when he said, 'Your children are not your children / They are the sons and daughters of Life's longing for itself / They come through you but not from you / And though they are with you yet they belong not to you.'[18]

As a Head teacher, I find the greatest single problem with parents is when they try – they believe for good reasons – to make their children like them, to be a 'mini-me'. Gibran continues, 'You may give them your love but not your

---

[18]Gibran, K. (2012). *The Prophet: A New Annotated Edition*. Oneworld Publications.

VIII. Growing old need not be a journey into isolation and loneliness, even with infirmity and loss. *Growing older* can be a path to ever greater wisdom and joy.

thoughts / For they have their own thoughts / You may strive to be like them, but seek not to make them like you.'[19] This is the worst kind of parenting. It is narcissistic. Parents trying to live their lives through their children is deeply harmful.

Losing balance on recreation

If we do not give time to the process of re-creating ourselves then we become stale, dull and tired, and life becomes full of a dull ache. Lose the balance the other way and allow our recreation to become 'work' and overly serious, and pain will equally result.

If we take our sports team or our sport too seriously, then we experience pain every time our team loses, or we play badly. Let shopping become an end in itself, allow ourselves to become so obsessed by travelling that we cannot settle at home, or become fixated on our computer screens, and we lose balance: pain results.

We need to learn to travel lightly through life. This does not mean that we are superficial. Mindfulness, which I understand as an awareness in the present moment of our thoughts, feelings and sensations, with acceptance and without judgement or comment, can help us to find a bearable lightness of being. We learn to care, but not to care.

---

[19] Ibid.

Beauty as an obsession

An appreciation of aesthetics – in art or in people – is one of life's pleasures. But when we become obsessed by beauty and its pursuit, we end up losing control. Obsession with the object becomes a substitute for the development of our own inner life. We become enslaved.

Beauty is tremendously over-valued in our culture. Both men and women are obsessed with it – their own and their partner's. Since the financial crash of 2008, the world seems more obsessed with luxury goods and beautiful bodies than ever. This is a chimera, a mirage. It will not quench our souls' hunger for permanence, any more than it did in the time of the pharaohs.

One of the secrets to living a more joyful life is to understand that we can never really possess anything. When we realise that we can possess nothing, we possess everything. We understand that possession may be an illusion but connection is not: we are profoundly connected to everything. This realisation is a gateway out of pain.

Understanding our own pain

It is important to reflect on pain. If we understand its causes better we are less likely to suffer from it. We have been examining the way in which pleasures, gone wrong, can lead to pain. Use this as a starting point to explore the things that cause you suffering in your own life. They might be anything from that injury you picked up playing tennis, to the guilt you experience when you think of an ex-partner you cheated on, to the sense of resentment you still feel towards a parent. List below five painful experiences in your past or present.

Sources of pain
1
2
3
4
5

Write down now your strategies for minimising or eliminating this pain. This is asking a lot; no one can pretend it will be easy. But as we can all acknowledge, unconfronted pain does not go away and, at an appropriate time, we need to learn to tackle it head on, to acknowledge it, even to befriend it. In my own life, some of the most painful experiences have come from a sense of letting myself down, or letting down those I have loved, especially my parents. Even more acute has been the pain of rejection: of unreciprocated love or love rebuffed. Learning how to sit with our pain rather than hide from it will provide important clues to our release.

	Source of pain	Strategy for amelioration
1		
2		
3		
4		
5		

Note whether your strategies involve suppression or denial of the pain, or work towards an acceptance of it. The former approach will reduce the immediate sting but will not remove the root cause. Embracing that cause and resolving to move beyond this inevitably self-centred concern towards an active and positive relationship with others, will help you move beyond the pain. This is a lifetime's work but there is no better day to begin.

PART III

Happiness

'To see a World in a Grain of Sand
And a Heaven in a Wild Flower,
Hold Infinity in the palm of your hand
And Eternity in a hour.'

William Blake, 'Auguries of Innocence'

Why Happiness Matters

So pleasure is different to happiness. The former is an experience that comes and goes, that is dependent on a stimulus. Pleasure is a state of *having*. Happiness is a state of *being*. Pleasure flaunts itself and repels other people; happiness attracts them. We directly seek out pleasure but we can only indirectly seek happiness as a by-product of a life well-led. Happiness is an emotional state and cannot be induced by sense-stimuli alone. Repeated pleasure can certainly induce a happy state, but it will not be a stable one. Happiness is much more than an agglomeration of pricks of pleasure. It is a portmanteau state that conditions our whole outlook on life and the way we interpret the world.

The happier we become, the more energy we have, the more committed we feel and the more we engage with others. The less happy we are, the more the energy is sucked out of us. Life becomes heavy and dull and even simple tasks become an effort.

Happiness v 'happiness'

The 'happiness' referred to in this book differs from the term as it is used in positive psychology. Here, it is a by-product resulting from a moral life. I am convinced that happiness emerges when we live in respectful relationships with others and with our deepest and most principled selves. It is a richer and more fulfilling experience either than mere pleasure or happiness as it is conventionally understood by positive psychologists.

To achieve this kind of happiness requires conscious work. The more we grow into our true selves, the happier we become. Happiness is a necessary stage on our journey in life. We need to become responsible members of society, loyal friends and family members, good people working in jobs that ideally fulfil us. When we achieve this, we experience happiness. It is a stable and highly rewarding state, even if eventually we will be aiming to move beyond happiness to joy.[20]

Why happiness is not a selfish aim

Making ourselves happier is neither self-centred nor selfish. Indeed, being unhappy drags down everyone around us,

---

[20]This thinking owes much to the work of Richard Rohr: Rohr, R. (2011). *Falling Upward: A Spirituality for the Two Halves of Life.* John Wiley & Sons.

especially those who love us, whereas being happy gives them a boost. It could be said that we have a duty to live in a way that makes us happier.

Happiness matters on an individual level and it matters very much in families, but it is also crucial at a more institutional level. The success of organisations is critically dependent upon the contentment of its members, and in particular its leaders. An unhappy leader, who is at war with him or herself can make life a misery for everyone else.

The cost of unhappiness is borne heavily by health services. Depression and anxiety are widespread all over the world, and result in so much incapacity, illness and inability to work. In 2012, there were some 40 million prescriptions in Britain alone for antidepressants.[21] Depression and anxiety among the young are increasing significantly, and the age at which such illnesses manifest has fallen sharply.

The pursuit of pleasure may be seen by some as self-indulgent. The pursuit of a good life that results in happiness, on the other hand, is immune from legitimate criticism.

Levels of happiness

Happiness is a nebulous state but it is not impossible to quantify. Psychologists routinely measure it using a subjective questionnaire – by asking their patients how they feel – though

---

[21] Spence, R., Roberts, A., Ariti, C., & Bardsley, M. (2014) *Focus On: Antidepressant Prescribing Trends in the Prescribing of Antidepressants in Primary Care.* The Health Foundation and the Nuffield Trust.

increasingly it is also being measured objectively as ever more sophisticated scanning allows us to monitor activity in the brain.

In order to have a clearer sense of how you are feeling at this early stage in your journey, you may want to assess yourself on this scale below. It will allow you to assess your progress as you work through the book. The scale lists eleven levels of happiness from '-5' through zero to '+5': '-5' being the epitome of despair and '+5' the greatest exultation a human being can experience. The scale does not come from any particular psychologist or social scientist but rather it is based upon my own experience and reflections.

Before doing this exercise, focus your mind on what it feels like, for you, to be happy. Note down the five occasions when you have been happiest in your life, and in the right-hand column explain why you felt so happy.

	Five happiest occasions	Why you feel so happy
1		
2		
3		
4		
5		

The journey from '-5' to '+5' is a journey towards flourishing, inner fulfilment and radiant energy.

(-5): A life that is deeply dysfunctional, suicide a constant preoccupation.

(-4): A state of permanent deep distress, incapacity to function autonomously in the world, regular suicidal thoughts.

(-3): Significant distress and anxiety evident but capable of functioning semi-autonomously socially and/or at work. Periodic despairing thoughts.

(-2): Moderate depression and anxiety causing dysfunction and significant discomfort. Escapist pleasures such as alcohol and drugs are common as a way of suppressing these feelings.

(-1): Some anxiety and/or depression, either constant at moderate levels or periodically at intense levels. The pain is controlled by resort to pleasure.

(0): The person is functioning effectively in their relationships and at work. Periods of pain and anxiety are balanced by pleasure. The '0' level is much governed by pleasure and pain; genuine happiness is absent.

(+1): Life is reasonably enjoyable for much of the time, although the person is heavily dependent on possessions/status/approval of others. Some genuine happiness is experienced but it is transitory.

(+2): Significant periods of happiness combined with a successful social and working life. Happiness is still not secure and is inconsistent.

(+3): Positive consciousness of being happy much or all of the time with a flourishing and successful life at home and/ or at work. This is the highest level to which happiness alone can take us.

(+4): A different realm of contentment is experienced, one which is spiritually rooted rather than being dependent upon worldly status, possessions or other human beings. Radiance and joy are occasionally present.

(+5): A life lived in joy, immersed in love, with an understanding that we are part of an interconnected and transcendent world in which there could never be anything to fear.

Most of us will probably place ourselves somewhere in the middle of this scale. On any given day we may vary between '-2' and '+2' according to factors often beyond our control. Here's a funny fact. You will find a big internal drive pushing you from minus scores to zero. Life is not pleasant in minus territory. But once you are in low-plus land, it is tempting not to drive further. External factors may be needed to push or pull you up to higher levels still. The grounds for optimism are that even those who experience a '-5' have every opportunity of moving onto the '+' side, even as far as '+5'. Everything is possible. Except for those who believe it is not.

A meditation on eyes

The eyes truly are the window onto the 'who at heart' we are. They allow us to discern where on the eleven levels of happiness everyone is. Someone whose life has been full of indulgent pleasure – food, drink, sex and drugs – may well have eyes that appear lifeless. The inert, dead eyes in the face of late photographs of Elvis Presley portray a '-5' person. He had everything, but he had nothing.

Contrast this with the eyes of someone who is a '+5' person, of great spiritual peace and wisdom. Their eyes radiate love, compassion and understanding. Such a figure is Sri Ramana Maharshi, the early-twentieth-century mystic. Maharshi had nothing in material terms but possessed everything.

The eightfold pathway to a happy life

Western society lauded Elvis Presley as it does today's celebrities and plutocrats. We are invited to emulate their lives, and many people, especially the young, do. I regularly ask students from all backgrounds what they most want in life. The answers are almost always 'wealth', 'possessions' and 'power'. Ask yourself whether that's what you want. Take another look at the eyes in the photos above and be honest about your motivation.

This can be painful. It certainly was for me. I have had to force myself to abandon my fascination with objects of pleasure, status and power in order to go in search of what is of real value. Any transformation that has occurred has been hard-fought for.

We need to work to improve the quality of our living, we need to act deliberately if we are to attain higher levels of happiness. In my own life I have made use of eight different paths that lead to greater happiness and fulfilment. They are drawn from the wisdom of millennia and blended with observations I have made about my own experience. I believe they are ways of living better. They provide the signposts to living richer, more fulfilling and more moral lives. Living like this will take you all the way to '+3'. To attain levels '+4' and '+5' on an enduring as opposed to an occasional basis, something further and more demanding is required. That is work of Part IV of the book, work that will take us beyond happiness to joy.

- **ACCEPTING** ourselves and others will improve our relationships and bring greater honesty and depth into our lives.
- **BELONGING** to good organisations and being part of something bigger than ourselves makes us feel connected and reduces isolation, which is such a potent source of unhappiness.
- **CHARACTER** virtues help us live more moral and fulfilling lives.
- **DISCIPLINE** is vital to strengthen our resilience and to help us live in accord with our aims and values.
- **EMPATHISING** and showing compassion and appreciation to all deepens our relationships and enriches our lives.
- **FOCUSING** on our goals and the search for meaning is essential if our lives are not to be aimless.
- **GIVING** to and serving others elevates and energises us.
- **HEALTHY** minds, bodies and emotions maximise our opportunities for experiencing happiness.

Perhaps this all sounds like very demanding work. These strategies for living will rarely feel like the easy option, especially until we have built up the habit of incorporating them into our lives. But I can assure you that they bring huge rewards: the journey is enjoyable. Besides, what is the alternative?

IX. Appealing to *higher powers* may assist your journey to meaning and reality. Doing so can help addicts recover. The help is always compassionate, even if the path may be rocky.

2.

Acceptance

'Strive, change, perfect yourself.' These are the mantras that govern our busy lives. There can be much sense in them, too, although they need to be tempered and balanced by a healthy acceptance of our personalities and lives as they really are. Above all, we need to accept those things that we cannot change. As the 'Serenity Prayer' says, 'Give us the serenity to accept what cannot be changed, the courage to change what can, and the wisdom to know the one from the other.'[22]

Lack of acceptance lies at the heart of so much unhappiness. As we go about our days, there is a multiplex cinema's worth of activity constantly running in our brains, mostly unknown to us consciously, that is full of self-destructive criticism of who we are and what we are doing. The films are telling us we are crap.

---

[22] Shapiro, F.R., Them, Q., & Niebuhr, R. (2008). Who Wrote The Serenity Prayer? New Haven, *Yale Alumni Magazine*, 71(6).

Accepting ourselves

We belittle ourselves. We tell ourselves we're frauds, super-ficial, insecure. (You provide the put-downs; you will no doubt have some choice ones of your own.) We belittle our achieve-ments, looking over our shoulder at those we think are smarter or have done better than us, at an earlier age, and have more money or status. We belittle our possessions: our homes are too small or in the wrong part of town, our cars are not the latest model, our phones and gadgets (which we can't use properly anyway) are out of date. We belittle our relationships: our lives would be so much better if only our families were different, our parents less intrusive or remote, our siblings more sympathetic and our children, well, simply better.

Life would be just perfect if only everything were as we want it to be. Meanwhile, our failure to accept the reality of our lives makes us restless, dissatisfied, disillusioned.

For much of my life I've been very hard on myself. Take my height: less than five foot six. I've always minded being small. When I was young it handicapped me at sport, being in the 'in crowd', and with girls. I have a hundred vivid photo-graphs in my head of girls I reckoned quite liked me when we were sitting down. I got very familiar with a certain look of disappointment that crossed their faces when we stood up. Had a leg-transplant been on offer, I'd have gone for it. Boob-transplants are two a penny, I reasoned, so why not legs? I resorted to making endless jokes about my diminutive height as a way of bolstering my self-esteem. I've had to summon a sense of humour to cope with being a headmaster whose students, including the girls, all tower above me. Joanna and I were thrilled when we went to China for the first time in 2005, when we were no longer the smallest in the room. But lately the Chinese seem to have got taller, too.

Then there are my ears, which stick out. My older brothers jibed I would have been a good runner if it hadn't been for the wind resistance they caused. For years afterwards I would find myself trying to press them back at moments of low confidence. They were nothing compared to my nose. It went on and on . . .

I rued my inadequate brain even more. It was never as capacious, as quick or as profound as that of the people I admired. Whole swathes of human knowledge, including maths, languages and economics, were frustratingly difficult to understand. It pained me to watch as my friends sailed through their exams on cue.

Now I look back and think, what a waste of energy. So much anguish about things I couldn't change served no purpose and made me very miserable. Accepting ourselves is the first step on the path to happiness. We need to learn to love ourselves, and most people, including those with highly developed intellects, are very poor at it. I have found it hard. By beating myself up for most of my life about what I was not good at, I stopped myself from enjoying and celebrating what I could do.

Self-love and narcissism

'Hang on,' some might say, 'isn't self-criticism necessary? Isn't accepting and loving oneself narcissistic?' Let's see. As defined by Sigmund Freud in his 1914 essay,[23] a 'narcissistic personality disorder' indicates an inflated idea of our own importance and an unwillingness or inability to empathise with others. Narcissistic people are self-centred, self-referencing, poor at friendship and untrustworthy at work.

Ten years after Freud wrote his paper, the Jewish theologian Martin Buber published his seminal essay 'I and Thou'[24] in which he observed that narcissism leads us to treat others, not as human beings and as our equals, but as objects. In such a relationship there is only 'I' and no 'Thou'. The narcissistic personality is unable to connect with others; such people lack self-acceptance and experience self-rejection and rejection of others.

To Buber, the height of psychological maturity is when two people enjoy an 'I–Thou' relationship, encountering each other's depths and accepting the truth about themselves and each other as equals. This 'I–Thou' relationship is integral to the achievement of a mature personality, which begets happiness. Narcissistic people can only experience pleasure. Only those in an 'I–Thou' relationship can experience happiness.

[23]Freud, S. (1914). On Narcissism. *The Standard Edition of the Complete Psychological Works of Sigmund Freud, Volume XIV* (1914–1916): On the History of the Psycho-Analytic Movement, Papers on Metapsychology and Other Works, 67–102.

[24]Buber, M. (1958). *I And Thou* (R.G. Smith, trans.). New York: Scribner's.

Accepting ourselves physically and mentally

Changing ourselves can feel impossible, but often we make it harder than it need be. We much prefer to cling to our habits of mind, even if we suspect that they are detrimental to our happiness, rather than make the plunge into change. Many of us carry hurts and self-criticism with us throughout our entire lives, constantly diminishing our capacity for happiness and love. Sometimes, our self-limitations endure all the way to the grave.

Parents can do more damage to their children than anyone, abusing us with too much love and giving us an inflated idea of our own importance, or denying us love and crippling us for life with self-doubt. But we all have a choice about how we respond to this legacy. Our parents have done what they have done, often for the best of motives. They have left their baggage at the station. We choose whether we wish to keep the baggage, or leave it standing there.

Let's start with our physical self-image. Rare is it for an adolescent not to be acutely conscious of their looks, weight, height and physical attractiveness. Many adults are just as afflicted. Some spend many thousands of pounds on cosmetic surgery, though, ironically, psychologists say there is no proven link between beauty and happiness. One, Sonja Lyubomirsky, is emphatic: 'It is clear that becoming more beautiful in the eyes of others will not make you happier.'[25]

---

[25] Lyubomirsky, S. (2008). *The How of Happiness: A Scientific Approach to Getting the Life You Want*. Penguin.

Or we can take a more effective and cheaper decision. This entails learning to accept that we have limited control over our bodies. Some things are worth making the effort with: maintaining a healthy weight is a good idea (though not at all easy to achieve, for many of us). Beyond that, a new hairstyle might pep us up, cosmetics too, though they are only cosmetic. But deep down we have to learn to accept our bodies as they are. Once there is acceptance, happiness follows.

Begin by making a list of those physical aspects of yourself that you feel that you, or others, do not like. In the right-hand column, by each of your 'deficiencies', write thoughts about how you are going to reconcile yourself to them. Most of us are very sensitive about our appearance. You may not find it easy or natural to make a list of things you dislike about yourself. Nevertheless, pinpointing our 'flaws' can be revealing. Sometimes the very act of writing them down reveals their relative triviality. Strategies I have found useful for overcoming my own body hang-ups include humour and reminding myself that even if there are things I find aesthetically unappealing about it, my body serves me well. It allows me to do all sorts of things I enjoy, from walking in the countryside to embracing the people I love. Bodies are for doing, not just for being looked at.

	Physical aspect	Strategy for reconciliation
1		
2		
3		

4
5

It is perfectly possible to be small, or indeed very tall, to have a face which is not conventionally pretty, or to be above the recommended weight, but to still be very attractive. Beauty lies as much in our own eyes as in those of the beholder. The more we accept ourselves as we are, the more the beauty of our souls can radiate through every pore. Without inner beauty, external beauty is insubstantial.

Some of us suffer from conditions and afflictions that bother us, which you might also choose to list above. I suffer from tinnitus, a high-pitched whining in the ears. By learning to embrace the sound, acknowledging that it is present and probably always will be, I have found release: I'm no longer fighting it.

Much unhappiness is caused by our unwillingness to accept our personality traits and behaviours. Here there is more scope for change (though as always, the caveat applies – we must do the work to accept that which we can't change and figure out what we can), in particular by learning to adopt a 'growth mindset'.[26] The 'growth mindset' is underpinned by research[27]

---

[26] Dweck, C. (2006). *Mindset: The New Psychology of Success.* Random House LLC.

[27] See for example: Mangels, J.A., Butterfield, B., Lamb, J., Good, C., & Dweck, C.S. (2006). Why do beliefs about intelligence influence learning success? A social cognitive neuroscience model. *Social Cognitive And Affective Neuroscience,* 1(2), 75–86; Draganski, B., Gaser, C., Busch, V.,

which reveals that we are perfectly capable of changing the way our brains operate, that we can become more resilient, less prone to depression and self-limitations, and eager to embrace challenges that once seemed impossible.

This way of thinking is contrasted with a 'fixed mindset', where we believe we are the way we are and will never be able to change. 'You'll just have to take me as I am,' a common saying, epitomises the 'fixed mindset'. It need never be true.

We can only begin, though, from where we are, so make a note opposite of those personality traits you find hard to accept or would like to change. In the right-hand box, explore whether you might be able to change any, and if so, how. For example, some people worry they are overly deferential, too eager to please, shy, unable to speak in public, too afraid to travel in a lift or by aeroplane, or perhaps even leave home. Not one of these self-limitations need constrain our lives. Accepting that we have them is the first step, before taking courageous steps to let them go. They are all only thoughts in the brain to which you have become attached. They are not real. If it feels overwhelming to consider letting go of certain mental habits or behaviours, consider asking for help from friends, self-help groups or a talented professional. There is no shame in this, and in fact it may be the thing that sets you right on your journey.

Schuierer, G., Bogdahn, U., & May, A. (2004). Neuroplasticity: changes in grey matter induced by training. *Nature,* 427 (6972), 311–312.

	Hard to accept personality traits	Strategy for changing
1		
2		
3		
4		
5		

What about those circumstances and people you believe have hurt and limited you? These could be relatively minor things, or real biggies – don't censor your concerns. Whether it's the loss of a parent, the illness of a sibling, a relationship that has gone wrong, or a failure at work, put it down. Take your time: these are difficult and painful memories you're exploring.

We cannot undo the past, but we all have freedom to change the present by altering the ways that we choose to let these events affect us today. We need to accept that what has happened has happened and resolve, with all the power we can muster, and with the love and support of others, to move on. This is the only way to stop the past from continuing to limit our future.

List overleaf five circumstances or events in your life that you suspect have become self-limiting, and in the right-hand side, suggest ways that you might use to free yourself from their continuing hold on you.

	Self-limiting circumstance or event	Method to free yourself from it
1		
2		
3		
4		
5		

Ten types of acceptance

You may want to be kinder to yourself but not know how. So we conclude this chapter with some suggestions that you might employ in order to accept yourself more. Not all will work for you, but with luck, some might.

LET GO OF THE PAST
The past is over, finito. It exists only as a mental construct and only in as far as you give it energy. Living in the past, hanging onto what has gone before, is to live a life dominated by the unreal. It is no formula for happiness. People, possessions, jobs, experiences that were once in your life but are no longer, should be left just to be. Live rather in the present, with gratitude for the past, good and bad, and optimism about the future. Excellent professional help is available to assist us let go of particularly damaging and resilient memories.

FORGIVE OTHERS

The world is full of hate and resentment. These emotions lead to wars, destroy families, rip apart communities, corrupt organisations. Holding grudges and bearing resentments may or may not damage those whom you choose to hate but it will certainly damage you. Truly forgiving others makes you lighter and freer, brings closure and opens the door to the rediscovery of happiness. 'No cause, no cause', says Cordelia to her father Lear in Shakespeare's tragedy, an inversion of the father/child relationship in the Prodigal Son story. These are the most beautiful words of forgiveness I have ever known.

In some circumstances, of course, forgiveness is all but impossible. Where intense pain has been caused, perhaps through rape, injury or even death, it can be unimaginably difficult to forgive. We may need to forgive in smaller steps. Again, professional help or spiritual guidance can be immensely helpful.

FORGIVE YOURSELF

This can be even harder than forgiving others. We punish ourselves endlessly for mistakes we think we have made, for opportunities lost, for things done or left undone. Make peace with yourself. Close your eyes and see your own damaged self. Then see your strong self walking towards that damaged self and embracing you. Tell yourself that all is forgiven, and that you are now free to move on.

LIVE FROM YOUR STRENGTHS, NOT WEAKNESSES

Many of us are more conscious of our weaknesses than strengths. So uncertain are we about what we excel at, and so anxious are we to cling on to what we regard as our unique ineptitudes, that we thwart opportunities for enrichment. Celebrate the strengths of those around you, rather than alighting on their weaknesses, as we're all too apt to do. Highlighting strengths in others reminds us of our own strengths; criticising the weaknesses of others drags us down. Watch, and you will see it happen.

CELEBRATE YOUR SUCCESSES, NOT YOUR FAILURES

Dwelling on our failures, real and imaginary, is widespread. Rather than celebrating our happy relationships, our personal achievements, our successes at work, we beat ourselves up. Stop attacking your life and begin to celebrate more: be genuinely proud. Hear the voice of your parent or another significant figure praising your successes, even if (especially if) in reality they omitted to do so.

TRUST YOURSELF

If you do not trust yourself, then no one else will. Have you noticed that when you doubt yourself, other people begin to question you, too? Trust that you can make a success of things, and you will be far more likely to do so. Expectations are everything. Trusting yourself is different to being arrogant and impervious to the views of others.

BE YOURSELF

Stop trying to be what you think other people – perhaps a parent, a teacher, a partner, a relative, a colleague or boss – would like you to be. Some people may want us to become a 'mini-me'. If they do, they have a problem. Don't make their problem, your problem. Live each day from the very deepest part of yourself that you can access. Most of us work far harder at being the person other people want us to be than at finding out who we truly are. First, we must recognise this. Then we need to start accessing our deepest self. It will never happen unless you learn to live with yourself. Be still.

ENJOY YOURSELF

Do you ever feel guilty when you enjoy yourself, when you spend time on activities that bring you happiness? Can you even recall what really brings you happiness? The more you enjoy yourself (without hurting others) the more people will be drawn to you. Enjoyment is infectious.

RELAX

Most of us neither relax nor sleep enough. We are far better attuned at seeing how fatigue diminishes the performance and enjoyment of others than seeing this same syndrome in ourselves. Go to bed early tonight with a good book, have a bath or treatment this week, and take off next weekend entirely. Stop saying that you'll relax in the future. Relax now.

ACCEPT FEAR

Fears damage so many people's lives. We may barely be aware of all the fears that lurk within us. My own life has been plagued by them, though mostly they've dissipated over the years, all save that king of fears, the fear of death. (Though even that can loosen its grip.) Bringing them to the forefront of your mind is important because admitting their presence is the vital step to letting them go. Fear is merely a sensation in the body. It arises and it always falls away. Recognise the pattern. Fears are powerful because we choose to give them power. We can learn to cut off that energy. Once we have, the fears disappear without trace. Fears restrict us from becoming the people we are meant to be. Beyond fear lies happiness. Beyond all self-denigration lies happiness.

For some, as for me, therapy in its many forms, can indeed help us on the journey. Cognitive behavioural therapy (C.B.T) is the form advocated by Richard Layard,[28] and is supported by Action for Happiness. Recognising when you need help, and asking for help, are the first steps.

---

[28] Layard R. and Clark D. M. (2014) *Thrive: The Power of Evidence-Based Psychological Therapies*, Allen Lane

X. Probe all your *fixed beliefs*, mindsets, and commitments to ideology, including atheism. Judge less, and·be more open-minded and open-hearted.

3.

Belonging

Belonging to groups, sharing with and receiving from them, is important in our growth and is a potent source of happiness. Exclusion from social groups is a major cause of unhappiness, anxiety and anger. Belonging goes to the very heart of our existence as human beings. The parable of the Prodigal Son, memorably painted by Rembrandt,[29] can be understood as emphasising the importance of acceptance but equally, it shows us how much we need to belong, in the case of the returning son, to his family.

Belonging is a state that we often take for granted. We rarely think about the groups to which we belong, or ask whether our happiness could be enhanced by making more of such experiences, or indeed by terminating membership of groups that are no longer healthy for us.

---

[29] Nouwen, H. (2013). *Return of the Prodigal Son*. Random House LLC.

Why groups are important

Humans have belonged to groups from the very earliest stages of our evolution. Groups were essential for survival, safety and reproduction. The need for belonging goes deep in the human psyche. From the far reaches of our unconscious, we feel insecure if we do not belong.

Psychologist Abraham Maslow pinpointed the importance of belonging when he devised his celebrated 'Hierarchy of Needs'.[30] According to this model, basic human requirements for food, water and sleep are placed at the bottom of the pyramid. The tier above represents the need for physical security, health and employment. Belonging is placed above them in the middle tier of five. The only two categories he considers more important, at the apex of the pyramid, are 'self-esteem' and 'self-actualisation'.[31]

I have always had an ambivalent relationship with groups, wanting so much to belong to them and be loyal, while at the same time wanting to probe and provoke them to be (as I see it) better and more uplifting. As the Head of various independent schools, for example, I have provoked regular outcry among some of my colleagues by saying that our school sector should do much more to connect with those not fortunate enough to attend such privileged institutions. The hostility

---

[30]Kunc, N. (1992). The need to belong, rediscovering Maslow's Hierarchy of Needs. In Villa, R.A. (ed). *Restructuring for Caring and Effective Education: An Administrative Guide to Creating Heterogeneous Schools.* Brookes Publishing Co.

[31]Ibid.

and defensiveness from some – not all – in my sector has made me sad and ashamed.

Groups can be loose and informal, as in free-floating friendship groups or more clearly defined and formal, for example, our team at work. Either type can make us feel looked after and affirmed, enhancing and underpinning our sense of identity. We like to belong to groups made up of people whom we believe are like us. They remind us who we are and bolster our sense of identity.

Identification with a nation, a sports team or a religious group can be so strong that it controls our emotions (not such a desirable state – as always, moderation is key). When football teams have bad runs, some supporters become inconsolable. But when we are physically or emotionally vulnerable, groups become particularly important, ministering to our needs and bolstering our self-esteem and confidence.

From our first breaths on earth, most of us are able to take for granted the love of our family, who care for us with food, warmth and protection. Before we make any conscious choice in life, belongingness is thrust upon us. Our very survival would be impossible without it.

As we mature through adolescence, family ceases to be vital to our continued existence and becomes more of a choice, an institution that we elect to invest in, or not. Adolescents often go through a period when they need to reject their family as they search for their own independent identity; but if the family rejects them back, they feel pain and confusion. They demand from others what they are not for the time being prepared to give themselves.

Beyond adolescence, we choose whether to settle down with

a partner and create our own families. For many of us, this is the most potent source of happiness in our lives. Rejection by and exclusion from our families, through divorce, loss or breakup, can make us profoundly unhappy.

We inherit our families but choose our friendships. They affect us deeply: mentally, emotionally and even physically. They bring us great happiness and solace, when they work well. Exclusion from friendship groups brings pain and anxiety. Many people carry into adult life the pain of being excluded by their friends at especially vulnerable ages, whether at school or at home. Who does not remember such apparently trivial events as the party we were not invited to, or the group that did not accept us? Pain, depression and anxiety can result from such banishment and these stings are not necessarily any less painful in the context of adult friendships.

The British term 'to send someone to Coventry', the derivation of which is unclear, refers to the practice of consigning an individual to silence by refusing to speak to them. It is a peculiarly cruel punishment, a childhood version of solitary confinement. Humans are profoundly social creatures. Even toddlers form friendship groups. So do their mothers. At the other end of life, the elderly find that friendship can provide the deepest meaning and reward. Who wants to die alone?

The workplace can furnish a powerful sense of belonging; indeed, for many, colleagues are their most important social group, overtaking both friends and family as a source of happiness and meaning. We might wonder whether such people have lost a certain balance in their life, if friendship at work becomes all-important. There's no doubt, though, that the good opinion of our peers, superiors and subordinates at work powerfully boosts self-esteem and happiness. We feel a sense of buoyancy and security, knowing that our source of income is secure and that our skills and attributes are well regarded and rewarded.

Being sacked or feeling insecure about our career or the viability of our employer is an acute source of unhappiness and anxiety. Being fired or demoted can be the most traumatic event in our life. In the most visceral way, we are told we do not belong.

Pets and a sense of belonging

Living with a pet can enormously raise our happiness. Do they belong to us? Or we to them? Perhaps both. Relationships with animals can be every bit as intense as with human beings. For children, they can be key in their emotional development and sense of security. Animals can help us to become more fully human and to learn how to care for other people. In lives that sometimes feel as if they're teetering out of control, animals ground us in ministering to basic needs.

Our family has certainly benefited hugely from the presence of our pets. Our children's lives and happiness were deepened significantly by Toby, a much-loved golden retriever. A constant feature at our house at first at Brighton College and then Wellington, he had his own Facebook page and was invited to more parties than any person I have ever known. After he died, his red lead was left dangling over our banister in Brighton, while his ashes remained in a wooden casket on the mantelpiece. It took a year before the family decided we should release them on a cold Christmas Day, on Brighton beach. The ashes whipped out of the casket like a murmuration of starlings, tearing and weaving in the wind above the beach until they alighted upon a couple of young lovers secreting themselves among the pebbles: Toby's last piece of mischief on earth.

Our children were in their early twenties when Toby died. They were still keen that Joanna and I acquire a canine successor, which we did in the form of golden retriever Trevor. This dog grew and grew, until he became bigger than Joanna and she was no longer strong enough to walk him. He had to go, to a local family, who regularly send Facebook updates to our three children.

Rupert Sheldrake, the scientist and author of *Dogs That Know When Their Owners are Coming Home*,[32] claims pets communicate with their owners on psychic levels. Communication with animals can be extraordinarily profound and consoling. When Joanna came back first from hospital, Trevor, though only a puppy sensed she was unwell. He curled up by her side, gently protecting her. Whatever our age, we could all experience the comfort and joy that comes from a relationship with animals. They can cheer, console, heal and calm us. If you have never lived with them, you might be surprised by how strong a sense of belonging they can inspire.

---

[32] Sheldrake, R. (1999). *Dogs That Know When Their Owners are Coming Home: and Other Unexplained Powers of Animals*. Random House LLC.

Taking stock of the groups to which we belong

Many of us belong to more groups than we may initially think. Take this opportunity to list the groups, both formal and informal, to which you belong. Having done so, evaluate on the right-hand side of the table how happy the group makes you. Ask yourself, what you are offering to those groups of which you are a member. Is there more that you can give as well as more you can gain?

	Groups to which you belong	Evaluative comment
1		
2		
3		
4		
5		

Examine the list. Are there any groups that are no longer conducive to your happiness, or where your membership is no longer productive? How many of them are essentially comforting, and how many challenging? Our time is always limited, yet many of us play very safe in the groups to which we belong. Conducting an audit to uncover which ones are still productive and stimulating, is illuminating. We may find our friendship groups have become stale or toxic, or that we are members of institutions whose values we no longer fully support.

Now try listing any new groups you might want to join, noting on the right-hand side how you plan to do this. Be robust and imaginative, and seek out groups that will challenge you. You might choose to start Mandarin, take up sailing or scuba diving, begin yoga or tai chi, explore your own faith or philosophy more fully, take an art history degree or go on a group walking holiday in Norway. Sometimes we all need to break out of ruts and seek out bracing new experiences. Plunge afresh into the ocean.

Group you wish to join	Strategy for becoming involved

It can be powerfully liberating to join totally fresh groups. They don't have preconceived ideas about who you are, which means they won't limit you – as current associates can and do. You are freer to display parts of your personality that may be suppressed elsewhere and which are ripe for being opened out.

Much happiness can be derived from taking the initiative, forming new groups, revivifying worthy but inert ones and contributing positively to flourishing ones. No group is more important than your family. You might begin there.

Fractured societies

Richard Layard, the economist and writer on happiness, believes that current stagnant levels of happiness can be explained by the 'break-up of the family, fractured communities, and a loss of trust'.[33] The increasing atomisation and depersonalisation of modern society and the substitution of relationships and belonging by technology, has been in train for many years.

The syndrome has been memorably described by Robert Putnam, whose book title sums up his thesis: *Bowling Alone*.[34] The hectic pace of modern life, the decline of the nuclear family, the fear of violence, and social exclusion are all potent causes of the decline of trust and sense of belonging to a wider society.

High-trust societies and organisations are associated with higher levels of happiness. They share ten common characteristics:

[33] Jeffries, S. (24 June 2008). Will this man make you happy? *The Guardian*. Retrieved 17 September 2014 from http://www.theguardian.com/life andstyle/2008/jun/24/healthandwellbeing.schools

[34] Putnam, R.D. (2000). *Bowling Alone: The Collapse and Revival of American Community*. Simon and Schuster.

- **THEY** are grounded on ethical values, sometimes explicitly religious principles.
- **PEOPLE** within the organisations exhibit pride and a sense of ownership.
- **LEADERS** display a wider responsibility beyond the mere maximisation of profit and personal gain.
- **MEMBERS** have clear responsibilities and duties rather than just rights, and actively contribute to the organisation's success.
- **LEADERS** run regimes that help eliminate fear.
- **LEADERS** win over hearts as well as minds, rather than rely on fear and coercion.
- **COMMUNICATION**, within and beyond the community, is fundamentally honest and open.
- **THOSE** belonging to the organisations are well looked after and have their rights guaranteed.
- **THE** family is respected and supported.
- **THERE** is a human scale: individuals are known and valued as individuals.

To build a happier and more trusting society, it is necessary for individuals, especially those in positions of responsibility, to act in trustworthy ways. Trust is a quality that has to be earned: leaders who say 'trust me' are rarely trusted, because they are judged on their deeds, not words.

In our journey towards enhanced happiness, we need to have trust in those organisations to which we belong, and to play our part by ensuring that we ourselves become principled and trustworthy contributors to organisations, whether as members or leaders.

Solitude: from belonging to something to belonging to everything

In our journey to higher levels of happiness and meaning, we will reach a point where our belonging to groups will impede, rather than help our progress. Eventually we need to loosen our attachment to groups, not tighten it. In the process of becoming fully ourselves, we no longer need to be defined or identified with groups representing just one part of humanity – a club, a religion or a country.

A form of solitude becomes essential further on in our journey, as psychotherapist Anthony Storr beautifully describes in his book, *Solitude*.[35] Storr writes, 'The mind must make its own happiness . . . any troubles can be endured if the sufferer has resources of his own to sustain him.'[36] He believes we need to make our home deep in our inner being, ending our reliance on external parties.

For much of my life I have felt lonely, with my hunger for deep connection often left unsatisfied because of my own internal disorder and neediness. The solitude Storr talks about is not a painful solitude but a vibrant one, where an embracing of our own depths makes it much easier to connect with the depths in others.

Those who want to experience the profoundest levels of happiness, i.e. joy, may still belong to some groups but they will recognise that this need not limit or define them.

---

[35] Storr, A. (2005). *Solitude: A Return to the Self.* Simon and Schuster.
[36] Ibid.

Membership of groups was a necessary staging post on their journey, but ultimately they know that they belong not to a section of humanity, but to its whole.

Character

Our character is defined by traits and principles that guide us when we act and think. Every good act builds good character, and bad and selfish actions build poor character.

We are all responsible for our characters. The possession of a good one makes us happy while having a poor one makes us unhappy. This chapter will explore how we can develop a better character.

Money may or may not be the root of all evil (I doubt it). But coins were certainly responsible for the derivation of the word 'character'. The ancient Greek word *charakter* refers to the distinctive markings impressed on coins.

Aristotle argued that good character was based upon the satisfaction we derive from fulfilling actions, and the natural desire of human beings to form positive relations with each other. He believed that almost all of us are capable of becoming better people, the more that we act in accordance with our good character. He suggested that leaders need to spend considerable time preparing for the onerous responsibility of office. Good character traits needed to be fostered to ensure that, once in power, leaders would act with wisdom. 'Excellence is an art won by training and habituation. We do not act rightly because we have virtue or excellence, but we rather have those because we have acted rightly. We are what we repeatedly do. Excellence, then, is not an act but a habit.'[37]

From the age of character to the age of personality

The emphasis placed by society on good character waxes and wanes. Today it is not a fashionable concept, in part because leaders, political, religious and economic, are so wary of championing it for fears that the media will turn on them and highlight their own hypocrisies. Leaders the world over dread the 'character question' coming back to haunt them.

I think that's a shame. Good character is as much of a requirement for living a happy life as it ever has been. Poor character displayed by our leaders across the developed world has contributed to the erosion of trust in individuals and institutions and has had a corrosive effect throughout nations. The ubiquitous celebration of money, fame and celebrity, none of which are generally associated with good character, provides a poor example, most notably for the young, to seek to emulate.

Not that this is a recent phenomenon. A shift from people being judged for the quality of their actions to the way they present themselves came with the publication in 1936 of the

---

[37]This quote is actually by Durant, paraphrasing Aristotle: Durant, W. (1961). *Story of Philosophy*. Simon and Schuster.

influential bestseller *How to Win Friends and Influence People* by Dale Carnegie.[38] Susan Cain has argued in her book *Quiet: The Power of Introverts in a World That Can't Stop Talking*, that this was the moment when the 'age of personality' took over from the 'age of character'.[39]

It has probably been exacerbated by shifts brought about by technology, though. The explosion of social media and the twenty-four-hour news cycle have helped make public figures the world over slaves to image. Too much of the time, spin wins out over substance. Principles have yielded to expediency. Imagination to image. Character to colour.

Teaching character

The best schools for the development of good character are families. Where children are nurtured in loving and caring homes, they have the best possible start in life. But we cannot rely on families everywhere to provide this example, and even where they do, schools have a key role of reinforcement.

For much of the twentieth century, the imparting of good character was widely understood as a core mission of schools. Particular emphasis was placed upon character traits including politeness, punctuality, loyalty, courage and obedience. By the late-twentieth century, schools the world over were shifting their focus overwhelmingly to the one objective of passing

---

[38] Carnegie, D. (1938). *How to Win Friends and Influence People.* Inktree.

[39] Cain, S. (2013). *Quiet: The Power of Introverts in a World That Can't Stop Talking.* Random House LLC.

exams. A body called 'Programme for International Student Assessment' (PISA), which produces international tables of school performance every three years, became powerfully important to national governments. PISA's measurements have had a positive impact in helping identify and root out second-rate teaching and poor leadership. But the drive towards exams as the only metric by which schools are valued has had disastrous consequences. Schooling has become reduced to a factory process of producing mechanised exam results, with teachers robbed of their professionalism and individuality, and students becoming passive learners who have merely to master the tricks of the exam board to succeed. Instruction has taken the place of education, and repetitive learning has trampled over liberal and broad education.

Schools do not have to be like this. The best the world over – in the United States as in the Far East – still lay great stress upon the development of character amongst their students. These schools are also some of the highest performers in international league tables.

By upholding, praising and rewarding good character traits including hard work, kindness, courage and loyalty, schools help students come to understand the behaviours to be emulated. This work carries much more weight when younger students can see the older ones holding positions of responsibility, and teachers and pastoral leaders themselves modelling these behaviours.

Schools and families are not of course the only places where the young can learn good character. The Scout movement, established by army officer Robert Baden-Powell, is grounded upon what he learnt when serving in India and

Africa about the importance of teamwork and the acquisition of crafts and skills. At the heart of his vision was the building of good character among young people, in the sound belief that traits developed in childhood and adolescence would remain implanted and a source of inspiration throughout life.

Religious bodies – churches, mosques, synagogues and temples – all have major roles to play in developing good character, above all by focusing on the need for kindness and consideration and providing opportunities for serving the needy in the community. At best, they do this very successfully. At worst, their adherents fall short of the fine values that they preach.

Our values and principles
set our character

Our character is shaped by our experiences and innermost beliefs, and we need to understand what they are. We can visualise our unique self as a flowerbed, with the flowers being our character traits, organically linked to the soil from which they spring. Traits we do not like can be viewed as weeds, equally emanating from deep within us, but capable of being plucked out and thrown away.

Being honest about those traits we do not like is far from easy. You might find it helpful to talk to friends or family, though even they might be reluctant to tell you, especially if they sense you are hiding the traits from yourself in your 'shadow' – the unconscious aspect of the personality that the conscious ego does not identify in itself. They may well want to avoid hurting or offending you. They may not want to damage their relationship with you. But explore you must. Your close family and friends will know.

Write down five character traits you do not like in yourself. Try not to be too self-critical. Perhaps they served a purpose at an earlier stage in your development but have now outlived their value. Take your time. Composing this list might take several weeks. Many traits will be in your 'shadow', hidden from yourself while obvious to others. Try to be as fearless as you can. For example, I find it hard to be told what to do or criticised and I can be unkind when I don't get my own way. I've undermined others when they've been in charge, while bitterly resenting those who do the same thing to me.

Once you have made your list, start to explore the ways you might reduce the salience of these traits, first by acknowledging their presence and seeing their hold in your everyday life, then by resolving to watch out for them fiercely, until, bit by bit, you pull out the entire weed, deep though its roots might be.

	Character traits you do not like	Strategy to pluck them out
1		
2		
3		
4		
5		

Your good character traits deserve equal attention. Draw up a list of five traits that make you proud, and which bring you happiness when you act from them. It may be instructive to ask those closest to you to draw up a list for you, and notice how closely the lists align. On the right-hand side of the box, explore how you might incorporate more of these behaviours into your life. They don't need to be enormous gestures. Countless studies have demonstrated that simple acts of altruism such as knocking on an elderly neighbour's door to ask if they need anything, are beneficial for both parties. As with flowers, watering and judicious pruning allows the plants to blossom with even greater intensity and richness.

	Trait that makes you proud of yourself	How you might display more of this trait
1		
2		
3		
4		
5		

One of the most important contributions of positive psychology has been the focus it lays on strengths. It gives as much, if not more, weight to what goes well than to harping on endlessly about what goes wrong. One of its most popular tools is the 'Values in Action Inventory of Strengths' question-naire created by Christopher Peterson and Martin Seligman.

It consists of a free on-line test, made up of 120 questions. It has been widely found to be useful in drawing attention to people's 'signature' strengths. I strongly recommend that you undertake this survey,[40] but only once you have formed a clear idea in your own mind of your strengths. The survey result will then either confirm or challenge your conclusions. Either outcome will be useful.

Knowing our own strengths is affirming and emboldens us to deploy them confidently even more frequently in our day-to-day lives. Every time we do so, our good character strengthens. The more it strengthens, the happier we will be with ourselves and with the world.

A life where there is dissonance between those character traits we advocate and the personality we project for others to see, or where time and care has not been given to ascertaining what our traits are, is a life that is dysfunctional and ill at ease. Good character matters. A life directed by our values is a virtuous life. A life directed by inconsistent and superficial values is merely a virtual one. We are indeed like a piece of soil. We choose whether to let beautiful and colourful flowers grow, or whether to be choked by weeds. We choose.

---

[40] It is available on the internet: http://www.viacharacter.org

Discipline

To fly, and to be happy, we need two wings. One wing is love, freedom, creativity and self-expression. The other is discipline.

I have just walked past a person of indeterminate gender huddled in blankets in a doorway by the River Liffey in Dublin. On the doorstep lies a bowl, pregnant for giving, but empty of notes and coins. This person will have been born amid great joy, or perhaps deprivation. We will never know. But however hard their life might have been, at some vital point along their journey, self-discipline or self-belief failed. I do not judge him or her. I see myself lying there. This could so easily have been any one of us under different circumstances.

Victimhood: Who is in charge?

Did this rough sleeper have any freedom of choice over his life? 'Of course not,' some will say. 'He was brought up in an orphanage, he committed his first serious crime at the age of twelve and from the age of fifteen spent much of his life in

XI. *Wisdom* and intelligence are different: seek both, but the former more. Education should prioritise wisdom, as high intelligence is no guarantee of it.

juvenile detention centres and then prison. He started taking drugs to combat his anxiety and self-loathing. If ever there was a victim in life it was him.' Is this kind of story necessarily true?

One of the core arguments of this book is that none of us need be victims. However hard it may appear, we always have a degree of choice. To choose is to be human. We may not choose what happens to us, but we do have a choice over how we react. We are today what we have chosen to be, no more, no less. We can choose to make tomorrow better.

The notion that we are mere victims is a product of incorrect and lazy thinking. The most important early contribution of positive psychology was the notion of 'learned helplessness'.[41] In experiments, psychologists demonstrated that animals repeatedly hurt by adverse stimuli develop a sense of defeatism, believing that they can never escape the pain. Some children and adults equally conclude, after a series of adversities, that they are incapable of improving their lives.

The key to abandoning the notion of victimhood is positive self-belief and a receptivity to change. Everyone can learn to be optimistic, to recognise that they can have personal effect and freedom of choice over their lives.

Pessimists take adversity personally and blame themselves, believing that the misfortune will continue indefinitely, become steadily worse and affect all aspects of their lives.

---

[41] Seligman's early work was on learned helplessness, long before he championed positive psychology. See, for example; Seligman, M.E. (1972). Learned helplessness. *Annual Review of Medicine*, 23(1), 407–412.

Optimists believe the opposite.[42] Pessimists are not preordained to be pessimists. With self-discipline, they can learn to be optimists. When they become tired of pessimism, they can make the switch. It will be as difficult as they want it to be. Pessimism has much in common with a 'fixed' as opposed to a 'growth' mindset.[43]

Psychologists have long accepted that young children who are able to exercise self-restraint will perform better in life. In a famous experiment conducted in the late 1960s in a primary school in California, children were presented with a marshmallow and told they could eat it at once or wait and gain a second marshmallow. Some gobbled immediately, others delayed their gratification. Years later the psychologists traced these children, now aged between twenty-seven and thirty-two, and found that those who had waited had 'a better sense of self-worth, pursued their goals more effectively, and coped more effectively with frustration and stress.'[44]

Walter Mischel was the psychologist who conducted these original experiments and has produced the encouraging news for adults, which is in tune with the growth mindset perspective, that 'the architecture of our brains is more malleable

---

[42]See Seligman, M.E. (2011). *Learned Optimism: How to Change Your Mind and Your Life*. Random House LLC. Note that other psychologists have a different view of optimism, such as Scheier, M.F., & Carver, C.S. (1985). Optimism, coping, and health: assessment and implications of generalized outcome expectancies. *Health Psychology*, 4(3), 219.

[43]Dweck, C. (2006). *Mindset: The New Psychology of Success*. Random House LLC.

[44]Mischel, W. (2000). *The Marshmallow Test*. Bantam Press.

than had been imagined, and we can have an active hand in shaping our fates, by how we live our lives'.[45] Our brains, in other words, are not immutable but can be reengineered by conscious work. At the heart of this transition is the development of the discipline of reflection and self-awareness, or mindfulness.

We can indeed be masters of our fate. Those who failed the marshmallow test may have to work harder at it, but everyone can exercise more self-control and discipline. Doing so will immeasurably improve our lives and happiness.

A disciplined life

We choose whether to have a disciplined life or to become victims – inert and passive recipients of whatever fate throws at us. Wise people choose to learn from mistakes and reversals, and to see them as opportunities to learn. It is an exciting and life-enhancing way to live.

I have always wrestled with discipline, often setting myself very exacting goals such as giving up alcohol and then beating myself up when I fall short. We should not be too tough on ourselves. It is hard work to change. Small steps can be easier than larger ones, and taking up a good habit easier than cutting out a bad one. But try we must. Even behaviours that we think only affect ourselves, ripple out to others. Smoking cannabis supports a whole evil drugs trade that results in the deaths of thousands caught up in

---

[45] Ibid.

its fight with the authorities. It also causes road accidents. Watching pornography alone fuels the exploitation of vulnerable people. We are all interconnected, whether we admit it or not, and we all have an innate sense, if we reflect deeply, of what is right or wrong. Self-discipline is like a muscle. We have to exercise it, and it will grow. The more it grows, the more dependable it will become and the less strain we experience when the pressure is on.

Observing those who possess strong self-discipline is instructive. Make a note of three people you have known at different stages of your life who possess this quality. On the right-hand side, spell out exactly what form that self-discipline took.

	Disciplined person	Form of discipline
1		
2		
3		
4		
5		

What can you learn from them? You may assume that such people have qualities that you do not possess. But that is not true. In every case, they will have worked to become the person you now admire.

Spheres of discipline

We are able to exercise self-discipline and choice over many more areas than we might think.

OUR BODIES

We have little control over the aesthetics of the body we are born with, but we do have control over the way we view our body and the way we choose to look after it. We decide how to rest, nourish and exercise our bodies. Our weight, fitness, body mass, heart rate, posture, cholesterol levels and much more are determined by our decisions. The Paralympic Games are inspiring because they show individuals exercising choice over their bodies even in adverse conditions. We can choose whether to become the masters, or the servants, of our bodies.

OUR MINDS

The incidence of mental illness across the world appears to be growing at alarming rates. Psychiatric hospitals cannot cope. Many patients have settled into their conditions, accepting the verdicts of medical professionals who, at worst, connive in making them feel helpless and like victims. In fact we have much more freedom over our mental states than many people assume. While some have inherited or chronic conditions, many of those who suffer mental health problems can ameliorate their conditions through the exercise of choice and will. For those not blighted by debilitating mental health difficulties, there are choices about whether to feed our minds with healthy and sustaining relationships and experiences, or whether to damage our minds with abuse of drugs, violent images and corrosive experiences.

OUR FINANCES

Micawber was right. 'Annual income twenty pounds, annual expenditure nineteen pounds nineteen and six, result, happiness. Annual income, twenty pounds, annual expenditure twenty pounds and six, result, misery.'[46] Dickens based Micawber, in the novel *David Copperfield*, on his own father, whose inability to control his finances landed him in debtors' prison. We can all choose to take responsibility to manage our own finances well. The result of mismanagement, caused by folly or greed, is indeed often misery, and not only for ourselves. I find it extraordinary that schools so rarely teach financial well-being – or indeed well-being of any variety.

OUR TIME

Most of us feel that we don't have time to do everything we want to but in fact, we always have choices over how we spend our time. While part of our life must be dedicated to work and to sleep, we have discretion over how we use much of the rest of it. We can all learn to manage our time better. Some do so: why don't the rest of us? Accomplished people manage their time well. They are worth watching. The key is being very clear about what we are trying to achieve – and working backwards from the finishing point. Envisage your perfect end goal – a house extension, a written assignment or a presentation. Then work out how you can best and most

---

[46] Dickens, C. (2001). *David Copperfield*. Broadview Press.

efficiently get to that end point. Being aware of your habits and how you expend your effort, often needlessly, will assist this whole process.

OUR RELATIONSHIPS

For many of us, our life experiences mean we are attracted to those who abuse us. But ultimately, we all make a choice about whom we want to love and spend our time with. It is a simple truth not always followed that some people are good for us, and good to us, and others are neither. When we choose our company wisely our happiness will grow. Choose poor company, and misery alone will result, sooner or later. Reflect deeply on the company you care to keep.

OUR ENERGY

We all have a stock of energy each day, like a bottle of water. We can choose whether to pour that water into productive places, to scatter it on weeds or to let it leak idly away, as when we become locked into futile personality clashes or bicker with strangers online. We rarely view the expending of our energy in this way. Neither do we acknowledge fully those activities that will top up our bottles of energy, such as having breaks, taking exercise or listening to some energising music. Stimulants like caffeine may appear to replenish our bottle, and will for a short time, but will only drain it more quickly afterwards.

OUR JOBS

Many of us feel trapped in jobs that no longer give us the satisfaction they once did. We may feel that our job has become simply a means to an end, and that we 'work to live'. But you may not be as trapped as you have let yourself think. You might be able to change so that you begin 'living to work'. Because work should be a source of happiness in all our lives. Are you working in the wrong department of a company? Are you working for the wrong company altogether? Or in the wrong industry? Or wrong country? All too often I have seen parents intimidate their children into making subject choices and career choices that are unsuitable for them. Careers are not about the parents' wishes, but their children's. If you discover in your twenties, thirties, forties or fifties that you are in the wrong job, take steps to change direction.

Doing so will of course be easier for some than others. We often feel that we are trapped by our responsibilities, to our family in particular. It is essential to take such responsibilities seriously, but might we not have more freedom than we imagine? Sometimes a tweak is all that's required to bring about a significant increase in happiness. Sometimes only a big change will do. I believe it is never too late to rethink your entire career. Even those who have 'retired' can take on fresh and challenging work, paid or otherwise.

Temptation and lack of discipline

Sooner or later we will all be tested by temptation: another drink before driving; a lonely and attractive person we meet at a faraway conference; a spliff or a snort of cocaine; claiming that meal on expenses . . . Sometimes the most significant errors we make in our life steal up on us ever so quietly and inconspicuously. We might even deny we ever made a choice, but we cannot deny the car crash, the divorce, the custodial sentence or the work scandal.

No one who is contemplating their life's ruins intended to end up in that condition. In every addict's life, for example, a pivotal moment occurred when they could have said 'no'. Every person whose life is controlled by addictive behaviour has made choices that brought them there. But the present moment affords an opportunity to take back possession of life. Every addict can regain control of events, however difficult and painful the journey back may be.

Alcoholics Anonymous (AA) was founded in 1935 in Ohio. Over the following ten years its 'twelve step' programme was consolidated into a tremendously powerful model of spiritual and character development that has had a transformative impact on the lives of millions. Carl Jung was a key influence on its development. AA's aim is not only to ensure a lifetime free of alcohol but to engender spiritual growth in each person so that they live a life that is more enriching and fulfilling than ever before.

Those who participate in the programme have to admit that their lives have become unmanageable, and to submit to a power 'greater than themselves' to release them from the grip. They make a decision to turn their lives over to God, however they may understand the concept, to admit their wrongs and deficiencies, ask for forgiveness, make amends to those they have hurt and, through prayer and meditation, deepen their understanding of the eternal. Many other bodies have modelled their approach on the work of AA, including Narcotics Anonymous and Sex Addicts Anonymous.

Acknowledging our addictive behaviour

You may be thinking, 'I don't have a problem with drugs or alcohol; I'm not an addict. This section doesn't apply to me.' I hope you're right and that you're not an addict, but even so, I would suggest that this section applies to all of us. We are all obsessed with something; we all do something to excess. (If you asked my wife, she would probably tell you I was addicted to work.) For some of us, our addictive tendencies are stronger than for others. Admitting to the problem is the first step in working towards a resolution. AA's twelve-step programme can be helpful in all sorts of situations but honesty, resolution and discipline are key in the journey to freedom.

Addiction can take many forms.

- **ALCOHOL:** a rising addiction, notably among the young.
- **BULLYING:** often to compensate for an insecure identity.
- **CONTROL AND CLEANLINESS:** an obsessive wish for order.
- **DRUGS:** both illegal and prescribed.
- **EXERCISE AND BODYBUILDING:** when it becomes an obsession.
- **FOOD:** eating too much, too little, or junk food.
- **GAMBLING:** made easier by on-line opportunities.
- **SEX AND PORNOGRAPHY:** which views others as objects for sexual gratification.
- **SHOPPING:** where spending capriciously is a distraction from other problems.
- **STATUS:** a social insecurity, where the hunger for status is an obsession.
- **THEFT:** often a cry for help, or an outlet for anger.

- **WORK:** where busyness is used as a way to evade issues or attain status.

What are your obsessions or addictions? List five. On the right-hand side of the table, note some ideas for how you might respond to them.

	Addictions	Tackling them
1		
2		
3		
4		
5		

Disciplined decision making

So often we react rather than act. We respond not thoughtfully but reflexively or automatically because our minds are hard-wired to react when certain stimuli present themselves. But there is always a space between action and reaction, even if it lasts only a split-second, for us to respond in a considered way. We have a choice, and to exercise that choice requires discipline. That space between action and reaction can be life changing. The most important decision we ever have to make could be compromised by an automatic response. If we had worked on that pause, we might have had the chance to act differently.

Imagine you are driving and you are cut up by a reckless

young driver. You allow yourself to get so angry that you knock over a cyclist who is then killed. Imagine hearing at the inquest that the 'reckless' young man driving the car was a doctor rushing to an emergency.

Finding the space for free will and conscious decision making is of the utmost importance, even in situations that are not matters of life or death. Regular practice of mindfulness allows us to expand our freedom of choice, in place of our habitual responses.

An important method for making more considered reactions and decisions was developed by psychologist Albert Ellis, with his 'ABC' model.[47] 'A' stands for 'activating event'; i.e. what has actually happened. 'C' stands for the 'consequences' of our response. What is often missed is the 'B', which is the 'beliefs' that condition our response. If we change our beliefs, partly by becoming aware of our propensity for habitual response, then we have a chance of altering the consequences.

Write down in the table overleaf five key moments in your life when something happened and you reacted instinctively in a way you later regretted. It is important to realise that you cannot have changed the 'A', i.e. the activating event, but you could have changed the 'C', the consequences, by altering your beliefs, the 'B'. As Shakespeare said, 'Nothing is either good or bad, but thinking makes it so.'[48] It is the *thinking* about what has happened that is all important.

---

[47] Ellis, A. (1994) *Reason and Emotion in Psychotherapy: Comprehensive Method of Treating Human Disturbances: Revised and Updated.* New York, NY: Citadel Press.

[48] Shakespeare, W. (1904). *The Tragedy of Hamlet.* University Press. Act II, Scene 2.

In the right-hand column write down how you reacted, and then examine how different beliefs about the initial action might have resulted in better consequences for you as well as for others.

	Action ('A')	Belief ('B')	Consequences ('C')
1			
2			
3			
4			
5			

Now imagine five plausible but undesirable events that *could* happen in your life. Place these in the 'A' column. Now write in the 'B' column your enlightened beliefs that might result in far better consequences, which you should write in the 'C' column.

	Action ('A')	Belief ('B')	Consequences ('C')
1			
2			
3			

4	
5	

The heart of the problem is our taking events personally, rather than philosophically. We need discipline to find the space to act with great objectivity. Compassion should become our guiding principle in all our reactions, and defensive egotism should be eliminated as a motive. Do this and we will find ever greater happiness in our lives.

One occasion when I drew on the 'ABC' approach was when I returned home after a tiring journey late one evening in June 2011 to find a note wedged in the front door telling me to phone the school doctor urgently. 'It's bad news, I'm afraid,' he said, 'you must come round at once.' He told me that Joanna had a serious cancer. My head was spinning. I spent the night feeling frightened and alone. But by practising mindfulness and compassion, I began to see the news in a more rounded and less egocentric way. My mind began to work practically to think what I could do to make the most of the circumstances that we now faced. Three and a half years later, after many prolonged visits to hospital, many tears and much joy, Joanna is still very much alive. The experience has deepened immeasurably our spiritual quests and love for each other. Adversity, I came to realise, is inevitable along our journey. It is our reaction to that adversity that is not inevitable.

Fighting back – resilience

Resilience is an invaluable quality that we can all learn to develop. It refers to our ability to handle adversity and difficult situations with equanimity, and to bounce back from them. Its possession allows us to come through difficulty without being too adversely affected. Low resilience means we are buffeted by life's misfortunes and setbacks, which costs our happiness dear.

Resilience can be learnt, especially when young. Children whose parents do not overprotect are fortunate. Such parents allow them to regain their own composure when adversity strikes rather than rushing in and comforting them for every tiny misfortune, thereby preventing their child from learning how to recover their own equanimity. Good parents guide and shape; they don't smother. The same applies to schools, which build resilience in their students not by sheltering them but by exposing them to challenges. Step by step, they learn that they can overcome difficulties and, in doing so, they build inner grit and strength.

List five recurring occasions in life in the following table that you find difficult to overcome. They should be events that cause you distress or upset. For example, I have always found it very uncomfortable to walk into a social occasion where I do not know people, and am apt to say stupid things as a consequence of my nervousness. On the right-hand side of the table, list ways in which you could imagine yourself displaying resilience to overcome them.

	Recurring occasion	Strategy to overcome
1		
2		
3		
4		
5		

As adults, we should be striving constantly to build our own resilience; we never know when we are going to have to draw deep upon those reserves. Here are some strategies for strengthening it.

- **AVOID ALCOHOL AND DRUGS.** Any kind of dependency makes it much harder to be resilient.
- **BREATHING.** Deep and regular breathing will allow you to calm and order your mind.
- **DON'T COMPARE.** Avoid talking yourself down by comparing yourself unfavourably to others.
- **DON'T FUEL CONFLICT.** Learn to be calm when conflict arises, and avoid responding with fear, anger or withdrawal.
- **DIET.** A nourishing diet allows you to face problems with much greater equanimity.

- **INSPIRING PEOPLE.** Read the works or look at YouTube clips of talks by inspiring figures.
- **PERSPECTIVE.** Recognise that few things matter as much as we believe they do.
- **PHYSICAL EXERCISE.** Seek out the most demanding challenge that's appropriate for your level of fitness.
- **PROBLEMS.** See them as opportunities rather than mere reversals.
- **RELATIONSHIPS.** Seek to extend and deepen those that nourish you.
- **REST.** Learn to sleep and relax better, recognising that we are much stronger when we are rested.
- **SELF-ESTEEM.** Associate with those who bolster rather than denigrate your sense of personal efficacy.
- **STILLNESS.** Extend opportunities for mindfulness and quiet reflection.
- **STRESS.** Learn to discriminate between acceptable and excessive stress, and to minimise the latter.

Many of these approaches have already been discussed in the book. When taken together, they make a compelling call to action.

Bouncing back: the comfort of others

We cannot become more self-disciplined on our own. The love of family, friends, even the comfort of strangers, will be essential. We may even find we need to open ourselves up to 'powers beyond', as advocated by Alcoholics Anonymous.

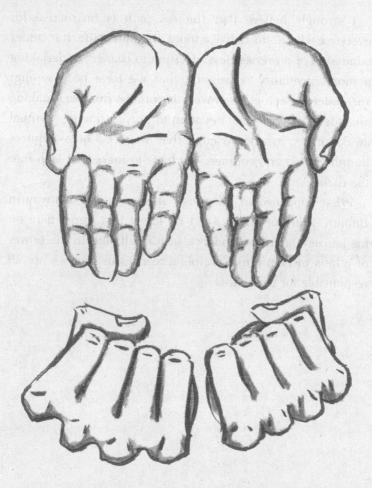

XII. Letting go of *attachments* to possessions, thoughts and feelings, especially in the 'second half' of our lives, is the way to the joy and reality that lie beyond happiness.

I strongly believe that the AA path is instructive for everyone who wants to live a more disciplined life. It includes admission of powerlessness; decision to change; undertaking a moral inventory; admission that we have been wrong; surrender to a higher power; becoming humble; making amends where possible; devotion to prayer; finding spiritual awakening.[49] To acknowledge that we need help requires humility, trust and courage. We have to make that leap into the dark.

What happened to the rough sleeper in the doorway in Dublin? I do not know. But I do know that somewhere on his journey he lost confidence in himself, and in the power of others to help him. Discipline teaches us that we are all responsible for each other.

---

[49]Alcoholics Anonymous (n.d.). *The 12 Steps of AA*. Retrieved 3 October 2014 from http://www.alcoholics-anonymous.org.uk/About-AA/The-12-Steps-of-AA

6.

Empathy

To empathise with others brings us happiness. Dishing out criticism and rejection leaves us isolated and unhappy. The capacity to empathise requires work, as many forces drive us towards judgement, towards detachment and cynicism. Of all human frailties, cynicism is one of the most destructive. It suggests a predisposition to be critical and a desire to impute the worst of motivations, even before the evidence has been weighed.

Expanding empathy, opening the heart

We have many reasons for not wanting to be open-hearted, including the fear of being crushed and rejected. So we hold ourselves tight, keeping our cards close to our chest. Not much gets through to us, and we give out not much in return. We do not have to live this way. We can learn to be open-hearted and empathetic while still taking care to avoid being bruised by the hard-hearted.

Try to identify things that make you feel compassionate to others. What moves you, what causes your heart to melt? It may be a piece of music, a memory, a poem or a passage from a book.[50] Make a note of what works for you, below.

What causes your heart to melt
1
2
3
4
5

Judgement and prejudice

Valuing empathy does not imply that we are denying the need for robust judgement in some circumstances. Professionals and managers are required to make judgements all the time. We have to assess who is doing a good job, whose opinion to value and where we need to intervene to make improvements. Criticism is inescapable and is not necessarily negative. Parents need to criticise their children to help them understand

---

[50] A book I've found particularly moving is *Black Rainbow: How Words Healed Me – My Journey Through Depression* by Rachel Kelly (2014) Yellow Kite. Rachel's subject is, in part, the power of poetry to make us more compassionate, to others and to ourselves.

the difference between right and wrong, teachers need to criticise academic work and behaviour so students can learn about quality, and all those in positions of responsibility need to be critical if standards are not met.

I am all too aware of the difference between healthy criticism and useful judgement, and their opposite. I've seen how schools can become corroded by an all-pervasive criticism. The younger children blame the older ones for not treating them better. The older children blame those younger for not showing them the respect they showed when they were young. All the students join forces to criticise their teachers. The teachers criticise the students. The parents criticise the teachers. Both groups say the school isn't what it used to be. Everyone – teachers, parents and students – criticises the management, particularly the Head. The Head blames the governors. The governors blame the Head. And in reality, as I know from personal experience, the buck stops there.[51] How refreshing if we had schools, places of work, groups and families, free of destructive criticism.

The problem with purely negative criticism is that it saps energy, corrodes goodwill and creates confusion and dissonance. All sense of value, purpose and principles can be lost. Everyone watches their back. 'Things fall apart; the centre cannot hold; mere anarchy is loosed upon the world.'[52] So said the poet W.B. Yeats. Jewish theologian Jonathan Sacks

---

[51] President Truman kept a sign on his desk that read 'The buck stops here'. Anon. (n.d.). *The Buck Stops Here' Desk Sign*. Retrieved 3 October 2014 from http://www.trumanlibrary.org/buckstop.htm

[52] Yeats, W.B. (1921). 'The Second Coming'. *Michael Robartes and the Dancer, 19*.

put it thus: 'be a do-er, not a complainer. Light a candle, don't curse the darkness.'[53]

A world of difference exists between constructive criticism, where actions by the criticised party have demonstrably fallen short of agreed guidelines and standards, and destructive criticism, which appears capricious and leaves people feeling denigrated.

Our constructive criticism will be more effective if, rather than the person we are addressing feeling that their whole character is being assassinated, we can convey that it is only some aspects of what they do that need to be addressed. Chilean researcher Marcial Losada found that successful individuals and companies make a high ratio of positive to critical comments.[54] Indeed, he says that if we want the person to whom we are talking to absorb our comments, we may well need to praise them profusely so they become receptive. Fail to do this and the barriers simply come up. The thesis has been criticised by academics[55] but the central theme of positivity resonates with

[53]Sacks, J. (2012, January 28) Ways to achieve happiness beginning with thank you. *The Times*. It is interesting to note that the 'light a candle' quote has been associated with many people, such as Eleanor Roosevelt and Peter Benenson.

[54]Losada, M. (1999). The complex dynamics of high performance teams. *Mathematical and Computer Modelling*, 30(9), 179–192.

[55]Fredrickson and Losada built upon Losada's earlier work (see Fredrickson, B.L., & Losada, M. F. (2005). Positive affect and the complex dynamics of human flourishing. *American Psychologist*, 60(7), 678) which was widely criticised by other academics (such as Brown, N.J., Sokal, A.D., & Friedman, H.L. (2013). The Complex Dynamics of Wishful Thinking: The Critical Positivity Ratio. *American Psychologist*).

the anecdotal experiences of many. Constructive criticism focuses on the act, whereas destructive criticism focuses on the actor. In the former, we can show empathy for the person who is being criticised. The latter displays no empathy.

It is easy to notice other people being critical. Others criticise, we *observe*. Those who are obsessively critical may be so because they are insecure. Confident and secure people do not feel the need to be constantly pejorative of others. We can all learn to be less 'defended', to be philosophical about criticism and not to spike back when we ourselves feel under attack. Better to learn to absorb the words, to listen to the criticism calmly, and sift out whether there might be material of value from which we can learn.[56]

I have never known anyone entirely without prejudice (which can be all the more destructive if not acknowledged). I do not exempt myself from this observation. I detect distinct traces of racism and sexism in my habits of thought. For example, I catch myself thinking in terms of generalised judgement when I hear militant Muslims, or indeed militant Jews, or the intolerant of any variety, including aggressive atheists, displaying prejudice to those they consider different and inferior.

List overleaf five groups against which, in the past or present, you have been prejudiced. You might be prejudiced towards workers or bosses, young or elderly people, Muslims, Jews or Christians, men or women, gays or people of other sexual orientations, even those who keep posing questions! On the right-hand side of the table, examine how you might begin to break down that prejudice.

---

[56] Walker, S.P. (2010) *The Undefended Leader*. Piquant Editions.

	Group	How to break down prejudice
1		
2		
3		
4		
5		

Prejudice can be seen as the flip side of belonging. We want to bond with those we think are like us: but that very categorisation means there are some outside our group who are 'not like us'. Much prejudice comes from deep within our unconscious and emanates from insecurity. It may be that empathising with some groups you identify above is too much as a first step, and you will first have to learn simply to accept them and respect their right to exist.

Rather than seeing groups en masse, try to see them as made up of a series of individuals. If befriending someone is too challenging, learn what you can about their lives and their difficulties. Start to see their humanity and you will begin to be free of your prejudice. Letting go of it is wonderfully liberating. Carrying hatred is burdensome to the mind and renders us heavy and negative.

Forgiveness

Of course, judgements are not reserved merely for those we don't know but don't like. Sometimes our sense of grievance is more personal. Many of us weigh ourselves down with hatred for individuals we believe have damaged us. Some of these sleights might be relatively small-scale: the lover who treated us callously when they tired of us, or the ex-boss who persistently failed to promote us. But some damage is much more difficult to forgive. Imagine trying to forgive the drug dealer whose actions led to the death of your daughter.

Make a list of five people whom you have found it hard to forgive, and on the right-hand side of the table, explore what it was that upset you about them.

	Person you found/find hard to forgive	What upset you
1		
2		
3		
4		
5		

Whole families, whole cities and nations, can be disfigured by hatreds and jealousies. Hearts are hard and people talk of never forgiving. They go to their graves unforgiven and unforgiving. This is a disaster. Hatred is fundamentally incompatible with happiness. A life that is full of hate can never be a happy one because the heart is surrounded by hardness and judgement, like a black lampshade that prevents all light from escaping.

No one claims that forgiveness is easy, though the longer the hatred goes on, the more difficult it can be to break through. Try to approach forgiveness in two stages. The first is to decide that hatred is no longer necessary or helpful, for us or others. We have to learn to see it as an unreal state that solves nothing and does not take us forward. The second, and harder stage, is where we seek reconciliation and build bridges, if the perpetrator of the hurt is willing to express genuine remorse.

This process of reconciliation has been used with significant effect in South Africa and elsewhere in the world. The approach has been called 'restorative justice', and has been found helpful by both the victims and perpetrators of crime. It can be used to great effect in schools and we employ it at Wellington College because it helps offenders to look into the eyes of those they have hurt and to recognise that they are damaging another person. This act of empathy is the beginning of learning how to be a human being.

We are all interconnected but we put up barriers that separate us from each other. When we see the other as they truly are, we see them in an entirely new light. Judgement fades away and we perceive them as just another human being, like ourselves.

In the following box, suggest ways of reaching out to the

five individuals you listed above, to allow a new relationship to form. Write the email, make the phone call, carry out the visit. Reach out from your heart and make the connection. You will feel an enormous burden lifted from the core of your being. You will feel lighter, because you *are* lighter.

	Person you found/find hard to forgive	Way to reach out to them
1		
2		
3		
4		
5		

Only connect

E.M. Forster's novel, *Howards End*, published in 1910, exhorts us to 'only connect'.[57] He was stronger on the injunction than on the method of achieving it.

To be empathetic we need to see others as they are in the

[57] Forster, E.M. (1997). *Howards End.* Macmillan.

present moment, to free our minds of any prejudice we may have about the 'type' of person we believe they represent, as well as negative feelings we might have about them as individuals. Mindfulness can help us with this process. When we truly see a person, when we can hear them, perhaps even feel the warmth of their body near ours, an extraordinary thing happens. Criticism falls away and we realise that the person before us is no different to ourselves, even though they may be more than twice or less than half our age, come from the other side of the world or live a social life of which we have no experience.

In such moments, feelings of love arise within us. Where once there might have been cold detachment, now there is only positive energy and a desire to accept, to listen and to celebrate. Connecting with others is a profound source of happiness. The happiest people I know are those who are most open, who welcome strangers and seek to connect with whoever is in front of them, regardless of sex, sexual orientation, age, race or faith. When we lead a life free of prejudice, we can see the world and other people as they are and we find happiness everywhere.

Appreciating life: experiencing it

We will never empathise fully with others until we learn to appreciate life. This is nowhere near as easy as it sounds. Most of us seem to be programmed to take life for granted rather than seeing it as a gift. As a species, we are extraordinarily adept at adjusting rapidly to change, negative as well as positive, and to returning to the same levels of happiness or unhappiness that we experienced before the change. Psychologists refer to this as 'the hedonic treadmill'.[58]

When I was twelve I had a powerful experience. I was excited for days beforehand and couldn't understand why the delivery was taking so long. Eventually, the big day came. Arriving home from school, the object was sitting in the corner of the room. It looked much like the old set, but I knew its potency was infinitely greater. All would be revealed at the pressing of the button. That night, the family gathered round, switched it on and there, suddenly, programme after programme, on television, in colour! I imagined that every day of my life from then on would be enhanced because of it. I felt a sense of profound betrayal when the following week felt much like the week that had preceded it. The colour set burst into life each night, but my life seemed no richer or happier.

Life needn't be that way. We can learn to appreciate everything in all its full glory. Moments of high intensity provide gateways to such experiences. For several weeks in the summer of 1974, long before I met Joanna, I spent every moment at Oxford in the company of a wondrous new girlfriend, and the whole texture of life changed. She was the lead in the first play I directed, and I fell deeply in love. Colours became

---

[58] See Diener, E., Lucas, R.E., & Scollon, C.N. (2006). Beyond the hedonic treadmill: revising the adaptation theory of well-being. *American Psychologist*, 61(4), 305. The term originates from Brickman, P., & Campbell, D.T. (1971). Hedonic relativism and planning the good society. In M.H. Appley (Ed.), *Adaptation Level Theory: A Symposium* (pp. 287–302). New York: Academic Press.

more vivid, shapes clearer, sounds and tastes more distinctive. I felt suffused by love for everyone and everything.

Many years later, a differently intense moment came when I broke the news to Joanna that she had cancer. I knew she was in a meeting with fellow teachers and I went to the room to ask her to come back to the Master's Lodge where I would tell her. I entered the classroom to call her and our eyes met. I think she knew at once. She recalls all the colours in the room, the stripes on people's shirts, their precise expressions, the sounds outside.

How can we learn to live every day with this same intensity, treating every moment of life as a gift and truly noticing what is in front of us? It requires a 180-degree change in conventional thinking away from taking life for granted to seeing everything, from fresh air to water, from people to animals, as special, a present. To make this change we need to slip our minds out of the 'automatic' gear and make a shift into 'manual'. I (and many others) have found that mindfulness is a key technique for making this happen. Even five minutes a day of sitting calmly and focusing on our breath can be enough to make us more aware of the texture of daily life and show us the benefit of learning to live more consciously.

Religion can also help us to make this transition. Praise before or after meals helps us to be appreciative, not only for the food but for those whose work was responsible for it arriving on our table. Uttering the words means nothing unless we listen to them carefully, in the present moment, and allow them to resonate deep inside us.

The Jewish religion is one of many faiths that has regular prayers of thanks, on every occasion, thanking God 'who has brought us to this moment'. As German Christian mystic Meister Eckhart put it, 'If the only prayer you said in your whole life was 'thank you', that would suffice.'[59]

The 'three blessings' approach, derived from religious tradition, is one of the most practical contributions of positive psychology. Christopher Peterson, one of its key protagonists, suggests, 'After dinner and before going to sleep, write down three things that went well during the day . . . Do this every night for a week. At the end of each day . . . after each positive event on your list, answer in your own words the question, "why did this good thing happen?"'[60]

A grateful attitude to life, whether informed by religious or secular humanist motivation, transforms our relationships with other people. It will make their lives and ours more rewarding. It will also make them happier, as well as making yourself happier.

Appreciating life: showing it

We like it when we are acknowledged by the fact of someone remembering our name. We like it when we are thanked, either privately or in a public forum. Being made to feel valued can be more meaningful than a financial reward. Receiving praise doesn't make us want to give up; rather it makes us want to give even more. Odd, then, that withholding approval,

---

[59] Meister Eckhart (1260–1328).
[60] Peterson, C. (2006). *A Primer in Positive Psychology*. Oxford University Press, p. 38.

affection and even love is remarkably common. We notice others doing it and disapprove; we don't see it when we ourselves do the same thing. We can always find a way to justify those occasions when we ourselves hold back.

We withhold that praise for a whole variety of reasons, including embarrassment, fear of rebuff and self-doubt. But we also withhold because we are preoccupied, we are lazy, or because we bear a grudge. Often, we are simply unaware of how much our approval means to others.

List below five individuals who have helped you. Perhaps they were teachers, or came to your aid at a difficult point in your life, or they helped you develop a new skill or confidence. They must all be people whom you did not acknowledge or thank properly at the time.

On the right-hand side of the table, list ideas about how you might still make amends by thanking them now. If they are dead, you could let their relatives know how significant the kindness was for you. It would surely mean a great deal to them to hear.

Person who helped you	Ways to show your gratitude
1	
2	
3	

4	
5	

Resolve to act on this list by systematically working your way through it and contacting either the people concerned or their relatives. You may want to write an email or letter or perhaps even make a personal visit. The important point is to take action and when you do so, to speak from the heart, without any thought about whether your message will be rejected or not. The likelihood is that your respondent will respond by saying how moved they were. Many retired people live alone, without ever fully appreciating what a profound impact their lives have had on others. There can scarcely be a more empathetic act than such communication.

In contrast to a sincere act of appreciation, a perfunctory thank you, a scribbled note or dashed off email, is almost not worth sending. We all receive countless Christmas and other festival cards scrawled with semi-legible writing. It is hard to feel much empathetic connection with the sender, beyond a compassionate feeling that they have been battling to finish their cards at the end of a long day in the run up to the festival.

As we have seen over and over again, happiness is a by-product of active, engaged and compassionate living. Trying to make yourself happy doesn't work but I can virtually guarantee that practising empathy does. Being empathetic begets happiness.

7.

Focus

Without focus we are like an archer who fires off his or her arrows in all directions, constantly buffeted by whim and prevailing wind. We may even fire an arrow straight up into the air which then lands on our heads. To find happiness we need a single focus, or sometimes a series of focuses in our lives. Without them we are aimless, like the indiscriminate archer. Decide where we want to devote our energy and we become a different person. We now have targets in our life, we direct our energies accordingly, and it will make us happy – as long as the targets have moral purpose and are respectful of others!

Finding focus

Many discontented people are discontented because their lives lack clarity and focus. They might feel that things have slipped out of their control, and that they are wasting their precious resources of time, energy and money on ends that do not chime with their goals. Perhaps they blame others for setting the agenda of their lives on their behalf. It can be hard to accept that we need not be servants to the objectives and ambitions of others. At every stage, life presents us with opportunities to take back possession of our lives. We can indeed become the archers, rather than targets for the arrows of others.

The journey into adulthood is a journey towards greater autonomy, with ever more possibility to choose our own focus. When we are young, our parents and schools give us focus. We are told to work for exams, to learn the violin, to play tennis, to be good and observe moral precepts.

In our later teenage and university years, the big questions and the purpose of our life preoccupy us. We sit around debating these issues with real moral fervour, until late in the night.

Then something happens to us. Work and children, among other things. Where is the space for thinking about our purpose in life when we are being woken three times a night to look after our children, and we have to leave for work at 7.00 a.m.? We lose our youthful idealism. We no longer seek to save the world. Rather we find ourselves struggling to get by, pay the mortgage, tend to the family, survive. For some, a mid-life crisis in our thirties, forties or fifties can be very alarming. But it might supply an opportunity to refocus on the big questions. If it results in us going forward with a new sense of purpose and direction, it can be a 'good life crisis'.[61]

---

[61] With thanks to Mark Williamson, Director of Action for Happiness, for alerting me to this term.

The imminence and then the fact of retirement re-presents us with a further opportunity to re-examine our purpose in life, an opportunity some take but some do not. A sense of our own mortality in our last years furnishes us with a final opportunity for fundamental re-examination. But why wait that long?

Taking stock of your life aims

Before we can re-engineer the purpose of our life, we must take stock of what is driving it at the moment. See yourself as the archer described in the opening of this chapter. In what direction are you firing off your arrows?

Imagine that you have five arrows in your quiver. Consider your focus under the following five headings: objectives at work, with your family, your friends, your home and leisure, and any causes in which you believe. In the box on page 156, write down your current focus in all five areas and, in the sixth box, write down your current overall focus in life. It is important that you describe the reality, not your aspirations.

If you are to aim well, you must clearly take account of the prevailing conditions. It will not be a formula for happiness to have unrealistic aims, which are beyond your financial means, your circumstances, or your physical and mental powers.

Without focus, we are like an archer who fires all his or her arrows in all directions.

Area	Focus
Objectives at work	
Your family	
Your friends	
Home and leisure	
Causes in which you believe	
Overall	

The longer you take to decide what to write down, the more likely it is that there is a lack of clarity in your mind. Perhaps you have encountered some resistance to doing the exercise: you may find it annoying or frustrating, or you may think it is pointless. Pointless is the last thing it is. Try to push through your impatience or doubt. The aim is for you to see clearly the point of your own life. It may be that no clear ideas form, or perhaps you are unhappy with the aims you have written in each section. On the other hand, you might take great pride in both the clarity of your thought and in the quality of your direction. If so, you are likely to be in a small minority.

Moving towards a clearer focus

In the exercise above you were asked to be *factual*. In this new exercise, the aim is for you to be *aspirational*: you are being asked to reflect deeply on what you want the focus of your life to be.

It is helpful to have a sense of a shorter- and a longer-term timeframe. In the middle column, list your aims for the next three to six months under each of the headings. On the right-hand side in the longer-term box, adopt a much wider horizon and try to think about bigger, potentially life-changing focuses.

Area	Short-term focus	Longer-term focus
Objectives at work		
Your family		
Your friends		
Home and leisure		
Causes in which you believe		
Overall		

You might well find this one of the most challenging exercises in the book. It is designed to make you reflect at a fundamental level on what it is you are trying to achieve. It is asking you to make your life more considered, more deliberate, more aware. Don't worry if you're struggling to do the work. There's no need to rush: thinking time is good.

One very effective way to kickstart this exercise is to try to imagine what you would wish you had done with your life if you were told you had three months to live. It's a confrontational sensation, imagining one's own demise, but it can be a powerful spur to focus. List below any new thoughts.

What you wish you had done

When you've completed this stage of the exercise, go back and have another think about the short- and long-term focuses you noted down previously. Do they still seem appropriate? Keep modifying them until you're happy. Thinking first about the short term is important, because you will only begin to adopt aims in tune with your deepest principles if you begin with the easier steps first. Do not allow yourself to be put off by the difficulties. Be strong. Take deliberate aim. And then release the arrow.

The journey to happiness is always from a reactive and ill-considered life to one where we choose to be in command. Fundamental to this shift is awareness, an acceptance of the truth of who we are and what is shaping our lives. That is why the themes of mindfulness and self-awareness constantly recur throughout the book. We can fire off arrows in all directions with no clear target in mind. Or we can choose to adopt very clear targets. But our ultimate aim in life is to realise that we are not just archers. We are the energy and awareness that flow through the archer, and the target is the transformation of our lives. When we realise this, our life will move beyond having meaning to having its *unique* meaning.

A seven stage focus model

I conclude the chapter with a model I use with students at school, to help them maximise their performance and happiness. It draws on several sources, including the 'Seven Chakras' and Stephen Covey's 'Seven Habits'. It is read from the bottom up.

CROWN – Be Still and Reboot
3RD EYE – Appreciate and Grow
THROAT – Optimise your Wellbeing
HEART – Empathise with Others
SOLAR PLEXUS – Take the Initiative
SACRAL – Manage your Time
ROOT – Set your Targets

8.

Giving

Kate, the wife of a fellow teacher, lives close by us on the campus at school. She regularly bakes cakes for Joanna, cakes which omit those ingredients that Joanna's cancer prevents her from eating. Now, why would Kate want to do this? She says that to give herself time to bake the cakes for someone else makes her happy. She doesn't eat the cakes herself, so how can she possibly derive satisfaction from this experience?

For me, the most eloquent statement about giving is the famous Prayer of Saint Francis: 'for it is in giving that we receive'.[62] But how we feel about Kate's gesture, and giving generally, depends on our beliefs about ourselves. If we see ourselves as isolated individuals, then our focus might naturally be on ourselves alone.

We choose many times over each day whether to make our own self-centred pleasure our primary focus or whether to engage and give to other people. From the moment we wake

---

[62] Nerburn, K. (1999). *Make Me an Instrument of Your Peace: Living in the Spirit of the Prayer of Saint Francis.* HarperSanFrancisco.

in the morning, our minds gear up for action. We can plot our trajectory for the day and decide whether our focus will be to minimise our pain and maximise our enjoyment, or to give our time and talents to help others. The former may bring us some pleasure, the latter will lead us towards happiness.

The nature of giving

If we choose the latter, what is it we might be able to give? Here are ten ways we might give to others.

ACKNOWLEDGEMENT

We can spend our days in our heads or we can acknowledge those we encounter, by saying a few words or even just waving at them across a room. This may be the only moment of genuine human contact some people will have all day. We often fail to acknowledge others because, by living in our thoughts rather than in the present, we do not even notice the people in front of us. It might even be innate to acknowledge others. Why else do we wave from boats to those on land? Why do we feel a lift when another driver acknowledges our act of courtesy on the roads?

ACCEPTANCE

Conveying to others unconditional acceptance is profoundly helpful and healing to that person, as well as to ourselves. It involves not judging ourselves, or others. For most of us, this is a stretch. Conditionality rules all our lives. We say, 'If only my partner were more attractive, my children more appreciative, my colleagues more friendly, if only I earned more . . .' '"If only" is toxic to happiness,' writes Jonathan Sacks.[63] Acceptance does not mean we are being unprofessional or lowering our standards, but it does entail that we can stop being so tirelessly judgemental. Our acceptance of others could be so much wider and more generous, and with that greater inclusion comes greater happiness.

EXPERTISE

We often define ourselves by what we cannot do well – speaking foreign languages, investing money, crisis management – rather than celebrating our proficiencies. We may be trained as lawyers, skilled at sport, talented cooks, effective writers, managers or carers. We can offer our skills far more widely than we do. Do not wait until you retire to volunteer your expertise: even those working full time could give far more. The rewards of sharing your skills pro bono may surprise you in their depth.

LOVE

The greatest gift we can give is selfless love. Love comes in several forms, as C.S. Lewis described them: friendship, family feeling, agape (or selfless love), and erotic love.[64] When we love we become fully human. To love and be loved reminds us that we are part of something much bigger than our isolated selves. This realisation always brings happiness.

---

[63] Sacks, J. (31 December 2011) Credo: Three resolutions for the New Year. *The Times*.

[64] Lewis, C.S. (1960). *The Four Loves*. New York: Harvest Book.

MONEY

Money is a store of future choices. We can spend it on ourselves. We can *think* we are spending it on others by hosting lavish parties as a way of showing off our power and ego. We can give it away recklessly. Or we can spend it wisely, on ourselves certainly, but also giving a proportion to causes where the money will be of direct help to others.

ONE-MINUTE STANDS

A one-night stand might be a recipe for short-term pleasure and long-term unhappiness. In contrast, a one-minute stand, where we help someone for a moment, by putting a bag onto a train, picking up an object someone has dropped or returning a lost item to its owner, will bring only happiness. The less you know the recipient and the more anonymous the act, the richer the quality of that happiness.

PEACE

We may not be able to bring peace to the Middle East but we can bring peace to our families and neighbours. Hostile relationships impoverish others, ourselves and communities. Make peace with all those you have hurt, and with all those who have hurt you. You will see yourself grow as a human being, and experience a profound happiness while doing so.

SMILING

Doing so makes others happy, and when they return the smile, it makes us happy too.[65] Frowning at others can unsettle them,

---

[65] Reciprocation of our smile is not necessary to increase our happiness.

especially if we hold sway over them. So smile at people, and notice the difference. Why is it that many people, especially intellectuals and high-status figures, find this suggestion embarrassing?

TIME

Giving time to others is about more than being physically present; it requires us to be mentally present, too. To give such time to whoever is in front of us, whoever they are, and to treating everyone equally, is surely the height of what it means to be human. We know how annoying and hurtful it is to be with someone who looks straight through us, eyes darting round our heads in search of somebody more important (though if we're honest, we may well have behaved a bit like that ourselves on occasion). As a teacher, I often see children suffering because their parents give them either insufficient time, or insufficient real presence when they are together. It is corrosive of happiness in the short term and profoundly damaging in the longer term.

TOUCH

Knowing who, how, when and where to touch requires advanced-level empathy, but once possessed, it is a wonderful

---

The 'facial feedback hypothesis' argues that the act of smiling is sufficient to increase happiness, see: Strack, F., Martin, L.L., & Stepper, S. (1988). Inhibiting and facilitating conditions of the human smile: a nonobtrusive test of the facial feedback hypothesis. *Journal Of Personality and Social Psychology*, 54(5), 768; Soussignan, R. (2002). Duchenne smile, emotional experience, and autonomic reactivity: a test of the facial feedback hypothesis. *Emotion*, 2(1), 52.

gift. Have you noticed how, when you are feeling down, angry or isolated and someone puts their arm on you, or maybe just touches your hand, some of the problem melts away? Physical touch is one of the greatest gifts and powers we possess, albeit little understood and too rarely used well. It is always a source of happiness when it is deployed considerately.

Predatory behaviour by some powerful figures prepared to abuse that power has helped create a generalised fear that militates against innocent touching, notably by adults of children. By innocent, I mean that the instigator has no ulterior motive and seeks no pleasure from their touch beyond bringing happiness to another person. With innocence, sensitivity and trust, touch can be a powerful healer and bringer of solace and comfort.

Still more so is hugging. Adults have much to learn from the way that young people put it at the centre of their interactions. I sometimes envy students at school when I observe how they embrace each other with a joyful innocence and lack of inhibition. How arid in contrast are the lives of many of their parents, who yearn for but lack that closeness. Often, their contact with friends revolves around dinner parties where the same stories are endlessly repeated and competitiveness creeps in, in the form of aggrandising anecdotes. Adults need to be like children or young people, hugging liberally.

There are many other ways of giving. But working with this list overleaf, write ideas for giving more under each of these headings.

Ways you might give	How you might give more
Acknowledgement	
Acceptance	
Expertise	
Love	
Money	
One-minute stands	
Peace	
Smiling	
Time	
Touch	

Whatever it is we decide to give, we offer this to four categories: family, friends, colleagues and strangers. Evaluate below how much you give to each, and explore on the right-hand side of the table whether you want to offer more.

Category	What do you give?	What more could you give?
Family		
Friends		

Colleagues
Strangers

Friends

We offer our friends companionship, comfort and compassion, but we can also challenge them. Let's dwell more on that fourth 'c'. We can speak the truth to our friends in a way that their family or colleagues may not. We can help push them beyond their comfort zones, as they can with us. Comfortable and consoling friendship can all too easily lead to complacency; challenge is *vital* in true friendship. Look at your own life and you may well find that your best friends are those who have pushed you furthest on your journey. Make a note below of the friends who have done this for you.

Three friends who have challenged you

Might we have outgrown some of our friends? Do we find ourselves repeating the same conversations with no real development? Friendship without growth is stale. Reassuring maybe, but arid and repetitive if not refreshed. How can we recover lost vitality? Perhaps going away for a weekend together would help communication on a deeper level than periodic evenings in the pub afford. Friendships need time to go beyond the superficial. How might you make new friends who stretch and inspire you with a new vision for your life? Might there be lost friendships from long ago – home, school or university perhaps, which you can rekindle?

We may have hundreds of 'virtual' friends through social networks and be 'friendly' with large numbers of different people whose first names and foibles we know. But it is likely we will be close friends with only a handful of people. There is no ideal number of friends, just as there is no ideal pattern to a friendship. What matters is that the friendships are fulfilling and rewarding, and that you both gain happiness from the company of the other.

Pose yourself these questions.

- Which friends have made you happiest in your life?
- Which friends make you happiest now?

Which friends made you happiest in the past?	Who makes you happiest now?

• How could you derive greater joy from their company?

Ideas for enriching existing friendships

Love and lovers

I have often been bruised during my life. I would not have
wanted it any other way because I have learned from the
rejections. I have never found it difficult to give and to love

others. I have always yearned to give the unconditional love that I felt I was denied when I was young. It might have been wiser to have been more discriminating but I have spent my life devoted to several people, to causes and to my work, using every drop of physical and emotional energy until exhausted.

Make a note of those people in your life whom you have most loved, noting whether your love was conditional or not. On the right-hand side of the table, make a note of those people who loved you the most, again noting whether that love was conditional or unconditional.

	People you have most loved	People who loved you the most
1		
2		
3		
4		
5		

What sense do you make of this list? Writing it honestly may bring greater understanding. Names on the right-hand side may suggest to you that some acts of recognition or gratitude may be appropriate.

How do we keep giving in our relationships, year after year? Why do so many partnerships grow stale and end in separation? Positive psychology advocates 'dates' at least once if not twice a week with our partner.[66] 'Mature' couples that have been together for several years may well not have been out on a date for months or years. Spending quality time and relaxing together with your partner, whether at home or away, is essential to keeping the eros relationship flourishing. It requires planning, imagination and commitment. The reward is obvious.

Do we give up too easily on marriage? The figures are concerning: there are some 125,000 divorces in Britain each year, with numbers steadily growing.[67] Do we do enough to prepare couples for marriage? For most of us, marriage requires real hard work: temptations are many while the rewards of fidelity can at times appear remote. While some married couples are not right together and go on to find real love with other people, others would appear to give up too readily. The Church of England offers some sound advice: 'Take stock of your marriage. Develop good habits, such as finding real time for each other. Remember what you liked about each other in the first place. And never, ever get lazy on each other.'[68]

Giving in families

Tolstoy's opening line of *Anna Karenina*, 'Happy families are

[66] Ben-Shahar, T. (2008). *Happier: Can You Learn to be Happy?* McGraw-Hill.

[67] Office for National Statistics. (6 February 2014). *Divorces in England and Wales*. Retrieved 12 November 2014 from http://www.ons.gov.uk/ons/dcp171778_351693.pdf

[68] Harlow, J. (11 November 2011). Caught in the slow torture of a semi-happy marriage. *Sunday Times*.

all alike: every unhappy family is unhappy in its own way'[69] is often quoted. The familiarity should not detract from the essential truth of the insight. I suspect that, despite this evident truth, a common misconception about the sameness of happy families leads us to miss the unique affirmation that can be derived from successful family units, regardless of size or composition. Happy does not equal boring. Far from it.

Over many years as a teacher, I have seen three patterns that happy families share:

- Family members respect each other. Parents have strong values but do not force them on their children to the detriment of their individual personality. Each member has a voice and none is allowed to be overbearing. Divisions, as when sons side with father and daughters with mother, are not allowed to become chronic. A strong sense of the collective prevails, yet members all feel they can be themselves within the family.

- Happy families ensure they spend quality time together. They savour the special events in their cultures and religions, birthdays, anniversaries and holidays. Even where they possess few material goods, each member knows how to celebrate and to enjoy each other's company. Older generations are always respected. Grandparents and great-grandparents are not treated as inconveniences but are revered for their long lives, what they have given the family, and for what they can still bring to it.

---

[69] Tolstoy, L. (2003). *Anna Karenina*. (R. Edmonds, trans.). Harmondsworth.

- A strong moral ethic, which may or may not have an overtly religious dimension, permeates the whole family. There is a commitment to objectivity and fairness, and distinguishing right from wrong. Commitment to the welfare of each member is mirrored in a sense of responsibility to the community. Typically, such families will be engaged in altruistic work together.

I have also found that parents spending time with their individual children alone is invaluable in keeping the bonds close. Some years ago, a school governor told me that he always took his children away individually for a few days each year. I tried following suit and only wish that I had begun earlier. I now spend a few days in the summer holidays walking with our son Adam, most recently along Offa's Dyke, which separates England and Wales and the previous year along the upper River Thames. As a family, we take our three children on a five-day 'mystery' holiday each year. They only know the destination when we arrive at a port or airline check-in desk.

Family life is of course fraught with possibility for hurt and it is unhelpful to romanticise it. Many of us, for example, carry a burden of guilt about our parents and spend long periods of our lives trying to please them. But if we are to find ourselves as adults, we must leave our parents behind. We can then come back to them and love them as they truly are. I know my own parents tried their best to love their children, and I regret that when I was growing up and for many years afterwards, I found their lack of inner peace difficult. My mother's ubiquitous anxiety smothered my maturation until I withdrew from her. I believe that in our last few meetings before she died, we rediscovered each other on a deeper level. As a parent myself, I regret that I was so restless when my children were young, and hope that I've been a more nourishing parent to them when my life moved into a deeper place over the last ten years. Only in the second half of my life have I truly begun to appreciate the intense value of family.

Many of us regret not having talked to parents and other elderly relatives about the family's history and involvement in national events, before it was too late. As a history teacher, I have always encouraged students to take an active interest in their family's story. They have prepared family trees going back as far into the past as they could research, and interviewed the oldest members of their family about their lives. This exercise helped the young people to see their elderly relatives in an entirely new light, and deepened the understanding of the intertwining of their own family's lives with national history. It gave a new way for old and young to connect.

Make a note of any ideas for how to savour your close and wider family. When, for example, did you last have a reunion not tied to a wedding or funeral? Families are one of the great under-tapped sources of happiness known to man.

Ideas for enriching your family members

Giving to colleagues

I am convinced that our colleagues are the biggest single factor in how we feel about our jobs. If they are trustworthy, supportive, loyal and fun, we are much more likely to enjoy our work. But we should not be passive, deciding merely whether or not we like and approve of those with whom we work. We should actively seek to give to them, by nurturing and affirming those who work for us, supporting and helping out those on the same level and affirming our bosses. Think again about whether there is more that you could be giving to your colleagues. If you have given all that you can give and you still find their company uncongenial, it is time to move on.

I am writing this book in my final year as Head of Wellington College. Joanna and I will miss it. It has been part of our lives for ten years. The Master's Lodge, our house, has been constantly bursting with pupils, visiting speakers, parents and colleagues. I am not good at leaving places or people and I am steeling myself to leave well. Every parting is, I know, a kind of death. The best way to leave is to think of others, not ourselves. A very difficult lesson to follow!

Giving to takers

What of relationships that have gone sour or are malign? They are huge sources of unhappiness. At work, it can be bullying bosses or aggressive colleagues; within marriages, abusive and hurtful partners; within families, it can be overly intrusive or negligent parents, or self-centred and badly behaved children. Is it right to hang on and fight, hoping things will become better, or should you quit, where you can? We all have a duty to be happy, and if we are being abused then we should assert our rights over the abusive figure.

To be assertive is very different from being aggressive. Middle-aged children can have their lives unreasonably curtailed by overly demanding elderly parents, or younger parents have their happiness and health destroyed by their children who have gone off the rails with drugs or alcohol abuse. Mutual respect lies at the heart of all good relationships, and where it breaks down, problems ensue.

I have seen too much of the destructive effect of drugs on people of my own generation. Elizabeth Burton-Phillips is a remarkable woman whose twin boys became hooked on hard drugs: it took the death of one to convince the other to give up. Now Elizabeth has dedicated her life to helping young people keep away from drugs, and helping families cope when their children do become involved. She believes in 'tough love', which entails asserting the rights of oneself and the family against the child who is holding the family to ransom. Her book, *Mum,*

Can You Lend Me Twenty Quid? should be read by all parents.[70]

Detachment is the way through debilitating relationships; we must learn to progressively uncouple ourselves emotionally from the person causing us to suffer. We may not affect their behaviour or stop their harmful actions, but detaching will steadily reduce the pain and allow us to recover our own life.

The purest giving of all

We have no possible motivation for helping strangers. With friends, there is often the motive of helping them as a quid pro quo. With family, we help in part out of a sense of duty. With colleagues, because we want to be well regarded and be seen to be collegiate and supportive. But with strangers? This is where our giving is at its richest and best, and where the rewards are at their greatest. Today or tomorrow, find a way of helping a stranger and ensure that no third party knows what you have done. The reward will be there.

As Kahlil Gibran says in the opening of his poem 'On Giving': 'You give little when you give of your possessions. / It is when you give of yourself that you truly give.'[71]

---

[70] Burton-Phillips, E. (2008). *Mum, Can You Lend Me Twenty Quid? What Drugs Did to My Family.* Piatkus Books.

[71] Gibran, K. (2012). *The Prophet: A New Annotated Edition.* Oneworld Publications.

9.

Health

Good health is vital to happiness yet we wantonly trash our bodies, pollute our minds and inhabit dirty environments. We need to learn to live naturally, by allowing our body and mind to function healthily, and to live in clean spaces. Observing animals is instructive when it comes to simple healthy habits. A cat does not overeat, it stretches, knows how to relax and keeps itself clean. What do cats know that human beings have forgotten?

Physical health

If the body is healthy, operating as it should, we feel happy. We are born with utterly remarkable bodies, capable of sustaining repetitive batterings and if we look after them well, they will serve us throughout our life. As with mental and emotional attributes, not all of us are born with healthy and fully functioning bodies. We may begin from different starting points, but we can all make the most of whatever we are given.

What do cats know that human beings have forgotten?

It has taken me half a lifetime to learn to live with my body. I remember a university friend observing that my body seemed to follow about two minutes behind me. I would arrive dragging it in my wake, always dressed in black, smelling of cigarettes, breathing slightly too heavily and with a distinct smell of alcohol. I resented her bitterly for saying it: we are often angriest when we suspect comments about us are justified.

No one would take possession of a car without first learning how to drive and maintain it. When it comes to our bodies, however, without which we cannot survive, we learn little about how they work optimally, how to feed and water them, how to oxygenate them properly and how to rejuvenate and rest them deeply. Unlike animals, we seem to lack (or have lost) an intuitive knowledge of how to look after ourselves.

Many of us claim to want healthy bodies. We devour magazine articles and books and attend self-help lectures, but our habits are often too deeply ingrained to shift. No amount of bias or even scientific arguments will alter us deep down unless the strength of our desire to change trumps the forces of inertia. For that to happen, honest and deep self-reflection is essential.

Consider when in your life your body was at its peak condition. Write down below five practices that you followed to maintain it.

Practice you follow to maintain your body in peak condition	
1	
2	
3	

| 4 |
| 5 |

We can all lead healthier lives: even those who are chronically ill have room for improvements. Your body is the way it is today because of the aggregation of hundreds of thousands of previous decisions, over many of which you had free will. Consider the factors that have led to deterioration from your optimal physical health described above. What choices have you repeatedly taken that have led to your body departing from its ideal?

Close your eyes and imagine your body operating at peak effectiveness. Write down five decisions that you repeatedly took that have led to departure from this ideal. In the right-hand column, write down thoughts about how you might change those habits and begin the return journey to ideal health.

	Decision you have repeatedly taken to depart from ideal	How to change that habit
1		
2		
3		

4

5

We all know the feeling of 'glow' when our body is at a peak. Every cell seems to ooze contentment, and a sense of harmony pervades the body. It may follow a long walk, some exercise or a deep sleep. That glow need not be transitory: it could be our permanent state. How might we make that happen?

Accepting and befriending our bodies as they are today is the first stage on the journey of transformation. From there, we can set about the work. To return to the car analogy: we need air in the tyres, oil to lubricate the engine, fuel to power it, water to cool the engine, regular driving to ensure that it operates properly and periods when we service and rest it to diagnose anything that has gone wrong. Each of these five aspects corresponds to core ways that we could better look after our body.

BREATH

We cannot survive without breathing, yet many of us do not breathe well. The very notion of learning how to breathe naturally, deeply and fully can appear alien. Yet actors, singers and sportspeople are all taught the skills of breathing rhythmically and using the whole of the lungs.

Once mastery of breath is learnt, we need never again experience fear or anger. It is difficult or impossible to feel either if we breathe deeply and rhythmically. Children should be taught the importance of breath control at school. They could learn how to sit calmly each day, breathing in to the count of three, and exhaling to the count of five, hands on the diaphragm feeling the rise and fall of the full lung capacity. Try this exercise now, taking several deep breaths in to the count of three, four or five, and exhaling to the count of five, six or seven. Practise it properly and it will transform your entire mood.

The more conscious we become of our breathing, the less likely we are to resort to cigarettes, cigars or pipes. The calm that we experience through deep breathing and the awareness of the delicacy of the process, may cause us to rethink the pleasure we might derive from the inhalation of toxic smoke deep into our sensitive lung tissues.

STRETCH
Oil is as vital for ensuring a car engine is properly lubricated as stretching is to loosen our body of rigidities and enable it to function properly. The body needs a good extension of every core element every day, ideally soon after waking up in the morning and each evening.

Yoga was practised for many centuries in the East and has become widely available in the West since the 1970s. Its ancient exercises are designed to help the body function naturally and at its very best. They are not muscle building, neither do they require aerobic stamina. They are simple, gentle and not competitive. Even five or ten minutes of stretching every morning will wake up the body, and allow it to function better for you.

When I first started yoga in the late 1970s it was considered very alternative, yet I loved the natural health of it, the way it made me feel so alive, and the whole lifestyle built around it with the emphasis on good diet, proper relaxation and deep breathing. You could say that *not* practising yoga, or similar stretching exercises, is weird because not doing so denies the body what it so demonstrably benefits from and needs.

We can equally learn to stand, sit and walk better. Doing so will reduce back and other bodily pain, while minimising the strain on all parts of our body. Some of us spend hundreds of pounds each year on going for massages, and revel in the pampering of the often very gifted masseurs who tend to us. But what we are doing is only the equivalent of popping a painkiller, treating symptoms, not the underlying problem causing the pain. In contrast, yoga, Pilates, the Alexander Technique and other similar systems will teach proper and natural posture to reduce the likelihood of pain emerging in the first place.

FOOD

Without fuel a car will not move and without food, our bodies will have no energy. The rule here is simple: eat what you know will do you good, in measured quantities, and at appropriate times. We have never been subjected to more advice on eating, nor more choice of food, nor more temptations. Food that is good for you need not be dull or unpleasant. Eating is one of the greatest sources of pleasure in life, and sharing food one of the greatest sources of happiness. Listen to your body. Imbibe what it needs, what nourishes it and what you feel proud to consume. Follow this advice and nothing else needs to be said on the matter.

DRINK

Water is the essential coolant for most car engines. Equally, our body needs a regular supply of clean fluid to operate properly. The best drink of all, where it is safe, is tap water. It may not taste great, look fancy or give you a buzz; but equally it doesn't cost you anything. Hydration is especially important if we live in hot climates or in air-conditioned environments. Our brains operate much better when our bodies are well hydrated.

Choice of drink matters. Additives, sugar and fizz: not good. They damage your teeth and the rest of your body. Alcohol is a wonderful enhancer, but ask whether you are controlling its consumption, or whether the alcohol is controlling you.

Many of us reach for painkillers when we should be drinking more water. Many headaches are caused by dehydration. Illegal drugs and even legal drugs designed to stimulate the mind should be avoided at all costs: all drugs bought at pharmacies, prescription or not, should be minimised.

EXERCISE

Cars need to have regular runs if they are to operate properly. Physical exercise for our bodies is equally necessary. Our bodies evolved over the millennia to be active, yet ours are the first generations to be sedentary for much of our lives. Most of us no longer grow or hunt our food, while in the West, numbers in manually tiring work fall year by year.

Our bodies crave the exercise that was once the daily reality of most human beings. We need to create our own exercise regimes. If we exercise regularly, we feel better, have more self-confidence and are less anxious and prone to depression.[72]

We should all organise up to three periods of exercise a week where we break into a sweat. It need only last for twenty to thirty minutes. It is important to find exercise that we enjoy, because it will give us the incentive to continue.

RELAXATION AND SLEEP

Cars need breaks if they are not to overheat and periods in the garage to be repaired. So do our human bodies. Many of us think we are relaxing when we plonk ourselves in front of a television screen with a large glass of wine. This is a superficial form of relaxation, and not conducive to deep sleep.

We can easily deceive ourselves about when we are relaxed, and become insulted if others suggest that we are not, especially after a weekend or a holiday away. Yet when we are genuinely relaxed we feel very different about ourselves, our lives and our work. What bugged us before no longer bothers us. Imagine you knew how to relax deeply, while still working hard and effectively. How wonderful life would be. Relaxation can be extraordinarily fickle; the harder one tries to achieve it, the more elusive it can appear. Learning how to relax is an art: but once learnt properly, it will never desert you.

Deep relaxation facilitates deep sleep. It is a cruel irony that the more we worry about sleep, the harder it is to experience it. Some people are lucky and fall asleep each night

---

[72] Scully, D., Kremer, J., Meade, M.M., Graham, R., & Dudgeon, K. (1998). Physical exercise and psychological well-being: a critical review. *British Journal of Sports Medicine*, 32(2), 111–120.

the moment their heads touch the pillow. But many have to learn good sleep hygiene. We need to relax for an hour or more before we go to bed, to find a pillow that supports our neck, to have a peaceful bedroom uncluttered by electronic technology, and ensure it has fresh air.

As with so much of happiness, we have to learn again how we were as babies, and how to soothe ourselves into the deepest recesses of sleep that allow us to face each new day full of vigour and optimism. Cats do not seem to suffer from insomnia; nor need we.

Armed with this information, write down actions you will take in all six areas to improve the health of your body.

	Actions you will take to improve this area
Breath	
Stretch	
Food	
Drink	
Exercise	
Relaxation and Sleep	

Healthy minds

The brain is a physical organ of the body, as well as the location of the mind. Like other bodily organs our brains need good food, air, exercise and rest if they are to be happy.

FOOD

Our brains certainly operate better if we eat good food, and our minds are also happier if we fill them with nourishing mental food. Material that elevates, delights and inspires should be sought, rather than that which cheapens, frightens or degrades our own sense of moral worth.

List five types of food you give your mind that elevates it and in the right-hand column, three that drag it down.

	Food that elevates your mind	Food that drags you down
1		
2		
3		
4		
5		

We choose what we feed our minds. Some choices can literally poison our minds; we then wonder why we are feeling heavy, bored and depressed. Boredom is always a choice. The world as it presents itself to us is never boring. But inert, incurious and dull minds respond to the world in a dull way.

Feeding our minds wisely makes us more likely to become immersed in what we are doing, in a state that psychologist Mihaly Csikszentmihalyi termed 'flow'.[73] He became fascinated by the activities of artists, chess players, rock climbers and dancers, among others, and noticed how they lost themselves in their chosen pursuits, all deriving immense happiness from them.

Note those activities in which you happily lose yourself. Concentrate on these and let go of those that no longer stimulate your mind. We all have something that we feel we should be doing, typically something worthy that we once resolved to take up. If you live in horror of your book group meetings, stop going. Do something else, something that fills you with joy. List five 'flow' activities on the left and five dreaded activities on the right.

	Flow activities	Activities you dread
1		
2		
3		
4		
5		

[73] Csikszentmihalyi, M., (1991). *Flow: The Psychology of Optimal Experience.* New York: Harper Perennial.

AIR

Teachers often let their classrooms become full of stale air, and employees their places of work, without realising that opening the window will allow their minds to become much fresher and lighter.

Inhaling fresh air is good for the mind. Notice how much more alive you feel after a walk, or leaving buildings behind and being out in nature.

EXERCISE

Our minds are happiest when they are stretched, challenged, engaged and creative. A vacant and inert mind is an unhappy one, prey to all kinds of idle thoughts.

Our schools and universities should have the drawing out of human potential and stretching of minds as their primary purpose. But the world over, they are slaves to the requirement to pass often quite meaningless exams. Teachers, not trusted to be professionals, become little more than machine operatives, implanting knowledge in a factory process of exam grade maximisation.

Schools and universities should instead be stimulating curiosity, creativity and active (as opposed to passive) thinking. The best achieve this. So could they all. The teachers we remember are those who have guided us into fresh understanding, who helped us realise great truths and insights and who fed our curiosity, pushed us and allowed us to be creative. Mathematics, foreign languages and philosophy are all stretching, and can be learnt by those aged ninety as well as those aged just five.

Those no longer in active work can all too easily fall into

a torpor of gin, gossip and grumbling. Keeping the mind stretched and creative, exercising it fully by reading and study, will extend life and profoundly deepen happiness.

REST

The mind can become so overactive it is unable to rest in the evening, at weekends or even when asleep. We have to teach the mind how to relax. The more we learn how to do this well, the deeper and more restorative our sleep will be. Relaxation is an art, which can be learnt.

List below five activities you habitually practise to help you relax.

Relaxing activity
1
2
3
4
5

Look at this list and ask whether it is as helpful as it might be. Alcohol, for example, is widely used as a source of relaxation and pleasure. But if we rely upon it we will come unstuck because though it may help us fall asleep, it will also wake us up. We do not sleep deeply or restfully after a few drinks. The same thing applies if we rely upon drugs, prescribed or not.

Books, films, computer games and websites may distract and divert us, but they will not all be relaxing us. Indeed, they may be agitating our minds, or merely distracting them from thoughts which sooner or later will need to be addressed. The key is finding ways to relax that are natural, soothing and harmonious.

Surrounding ourselves with beauty can relax us. Joanna is suffering another period of ill health and has just seen the film *Brief Encounter* from her hospital bed. She is full of the beauty of the story, the filming and acting. She talks with great animation for ten minutes about this timeless film we know so well yet still fresh, tears in her eyes, in a state of rapture. The experience has made her better than any of the several pills she has taken today.

List five activities you would like to embrace that you believe might deeply and healthily relax you.

Activity for deep and healthy relaxation	
1	
2	
3	
4	
5	

A healthy environment

The environments we inhabit – our living rooms, bedrooms and offices, our back yards and gardens – are outer manifestations of our inner minds. If they are orderly, attractive and full of beautiful objects, the result of choices we have made, they will help our minds to be calm and happy. An *obsessively* tidy environment, though, does not mean we possess very happy minds; it may, on the contrary, be symptomatic of an unhealthy mind.

Describe the state of your living room, working environment, bedroom and garden, if you have one. In the right-hand column, write how you would ideally like them to be. If there is a difference, note it, and ask yourself anything you may want to do about it.

	Description	Ideal state
Living room		
Working environment		
Bedroom		

Garden

It can be much easier to organise our spaces the way we want them when we move homes or offices. For a time at least, they become far closer aligned with our ideal. Then old habits return. Habits again. But they can be changed. Everything can be changed.

Redesigning our existing homes, offices, places of work and gardens requires an effort, but it can be done. Clarify in your mind how you would like each to be, plan out a budget and timeframe, then go ahead and make the changes. Make a commitment to ensure that your environment remains in line with your ideals. Doing so will bring you happiness, because you will be in harmony with your environment, because that environment is in harmony with you.

Go further. Have fun and imagine your dream home. Envisage the location, the exterior and interior, the rooms and garden. For me, it would have to be old, with a big open fire burning logs so that the smell permeates the whole house. The floor would be made of wooden boards, and the walls and curtains in strong natural colours. It would need to be near water, ideally by a stream, a lake or an estuary. Going to sleep to the sound of running water or waves is pure joy. My favourite architect is the early-twentieth-century English designer, Edwin Lutyens. He built in natural stone, wood and tile, using local craftsmen, so the buildings emerged naturally out of the soil, with the gardens and building blending seamlessly one into the other.

Happiness at work can be enhanced by aligning it, as far as you have leeway, with your personality. Display cut flowers or plants, postcards or photographs of people and places important to you. Working environments needn't be dull and impersonal.

Your clothes, too, are part of your personal environment. Dressing to please yourself is fundamental. Some of us do it naturally. Others talk to friends or seek professional advice. Some people never manage it, and look as unhappy and uncomfortable in their clothes as they do with their hair. Harmony is again the touchstone. Let your clothes be the outward manifestation of your inner taste and style.

It is much easier to be happy if we are in tune with our bodies, our minds and our environments. To say we have no choice over these is to say that our bodies as well as our minds are imprisoned. For many, that is exactly what they are. But we can all break out of the jail.

PART IV

Joy

'We are such stuff
As dreams are made on, and our little life
Is rounded with a sleep.'

William Shakespeare,
The Tempest, Act 4 Scene 1

Why Happiness Is Not Enough

If personal happiness were the highest level of being that humans could attain in life, then happiness would be enough. If people had not travelled to far deeper and more satisfying places, and if they had not returned to tell us about them, then there would be no need to move beyond happiness. If we did not yearn for deeper levels of experience beyond any consolation that material life can reward us, then happiness would be enough. But human beings are restless and many of us feel called to search out those deeper levels.

The remaining chapters of the book will take you on a path that will lead you beyond happiness towards joy. It is open to every one of us to find this deeper and richer fulfilment in life. I warmly encourage you to embark on this journey.

This deeper, joyful and spiritual vision of happiness is championed by Action for Happiness. Yet it is the self-centred understanding of happiness that is ubiquitous. Consider the following points.

- Happiness can be relatively superficial and prevents us experiencing the depths of which we are capable.
- Happy people can be complacent and self-regarding, as can those who work to promote happiness. When we speak of happiness, we are often referring merely to pleasure.
- Happiness can make us indifferent to the thoughts, feelings and suffering of others. We can become gated within our own happiness and idly assume that the rest of the world feels the same as us.
- Happiness can be stultifying to creativity and depth of human experience, because it contains rather than opens up our unconscious minds.

We saw earlier that, when we seek pleasure, we see ourselves as more significant than others. On the journey to happiness, others are as important as us. To find joy, we need to make others even more important than ourselves. We must not lose ourselves, but we must transform ourselves. We must move on, and we must do so without further delay. As Rabbi Hillel the Elder said, 'If I am not for myself who is for me? And being for my own self, what am "I"? And if not now, when?'[74]

I am now moving into unfamiliar territory. Whereas I have direct experience of the pleasure/pain and the happiness states of life, I have no more than intimations of the joyful level of being. We are anyway moving into a world of mystery where we have to leave behind certainty for uncertainty, the known for the unknown, and the rational world of the mind for a wider and more generous vision.

---

[74] Hillel (1939). *Pirkei Avot.* Vol. 3. CUP Archive.

The happiness trap

To be happy rather than unhappy is a worthy and admirable objective for our lives. If the eight paths described in Part III of this book are followed, then our lives will become happier. But the happiness that results must be seen only as a staging post on our journey through life, not as the final destination.

It can be a huge struggle to rouse ourselves to move beyond happiness. Leaving unhappiness behind is, in some ways, a doddle by comparison. We may find ourselves pushed out of unhappiness either by internal forces or by people around us. We have, after all, every incentive to escape it and to avoid repeating the unwise decisions that put us there. Most of us seek self-respect, stability and prosperity. Those who love and care for us want the same things on our behalf. Many forces push us towards at least living at 'zero' on the happiness chart, if not to positive scores.

But often we get stuck around zero, or just above, believing that we have enough. Material security and status can become a trap. We surround ourselves with our friends, family and possessions. Our mortgage is being paid off, our pensions are secure, our financial worries are over. We have achieved nirvana. Except we haven't. We may need to seek out discomfort, disruption and instability in order to bounce ourselves out of this false sense of security, and to push us further on our journey. Or it may be that, even if we don't go looking for them, these demons will find us out.

Religion can be another powerful trap. The world over, the

faithful attend religious services, they do good deeds, they live moral lives, more or less. But so many churches, temples, mosques and synagogues are stale and inert. They are run by religious professionals for whom the mission to inspire and instruct has become a matter of mouthing words; the spirit barely moves within *them*, let alone their congregations. Some of them preside over affairs in their own interests, while failing to acknowledge that that is exactly what they are doing.

It was against such self-regarding figures that Jesus produced his religious revolution. The sixteenth century saw the movement for reformation of what was seen by many as a moribund and hypocritical hierarchy. The church, and indeed all the world's major religions, are ripe for reformation now, so that once again they can be full of spirit, humility, love and joy. Religious institutions, at their best, are vital in helping us to understand that the goal of life is not happiness but joy, not comfort but meaning, not safety but boundless love.

The spiritual iconoclast, Jiddu Krishnamurti (1895–1986), spent his life warning against the danger of the spiritual aspirant becoming dependent on a religious teacher or tradition. His message was that only by becoming autonomous would we achieve our full spiritual depths.[75] His mission has much to teach us of the dangers of becoming slaves to a religious tradition and its leaders, rather than the active practitioners of its message.

Ideology is a further trap. The human mind is capable of thinking and believing whatever it wants. Any belief system,

---

[75] Lewin, D. (2014). Behold: Silence and attention in education. *Journal of Philosophy of Education*.

This book will take you on a path that will lead you beyond
happiness and joy.

including communism, atheism and religious fundamentalism, that claims it has a monopoly on truth is bound to be a limiting belief system. It might appear rationally coherent to its followers but it will be partial. The believers are trapped in Plato's cave, and do not even realise it.

A random universe or a grand design?

Human beings have choices. One is to see the universe as an entirely random occurrence brought into existence by a process beyond the capability of humans to understand. We may choose to view everything in it as the product of chance. On the other hand, we may choose to see only certain things or perhaps even nothing, as random. We may see a universe created with a purpose, ourselves created for a purpose, and our aim in life to discover what that purpose is.

We may believe that everything that happens is merely luck, good or bad: whether we are born into a rich family with health and great personal gifts, or born poor with few natural qualities. At the other end of the spectrum we may believe that luck plays little or no part, and that we are all born as meant to be.

We may believe that everything we do happens automatically and that free will is an illusion, because all our decisions are pre-ordained reactions dictated by powerful unconscious impulses. Or we can see nothing in life as automatic and everything as open to a degree of free will and choice.

We may decide that happiness (or indeed pleasure, or

unhappiness) is enough for us; or we can choose to look beyond them to profounder levels of human experience.

Many of us would probably claim that we settle somewhere between these two extreme worldviews. None of these positions is an easy option; they all have their challenges. But I am convinced that the way to experience joy is to shift our thinking in the direction of acceptance of design in the universe, and of the discovery of purpose in our lives. This doesn't mean we are meek in the face of injustice or adversity, only that we see even the most desperate setbacks as spurs to further exploration and growth. For example, even if we believe that illness and misfortune are random, we can decide to see every reversal, even physical ailments, loss of loved ones and destruction of our livelihoods and homes, as offering us a purpose, as events from which we can learn.

Most of us, even if we lay claim to the middle ground, are far more rigid in our thinking than we would like to admit. By the time we reach our mid-twenties we have adopted a mindset or world-view in which we either reject the possibility of the spiritual realm completely or embrace it (sometimes slavishly). Most people, I have noticed, are very reluctant to review their fixed position. I am asking for nothing less than a root and branch re-examination.

Jung v Freud

One way to understand this existential choice is to examine two thinkers who wrote extensively about the human mind during the last century: Sigmund Freud (1856–1939) and Carl Jung (1875–1961).[76]

Freud developed his system of psychoanalysis to help people minimise pain and maximise the possibilities of happiness. Jung's work was motivated by his desire to help patients find the deepest levels of meaning open to them.

For Freud, misfortune was simply bad luck; for Jung, misfortune can serve a purpose, to encourage us to look again at ourselves, to see how we can change our thinking and our actions.

Chance governs Freud's world; 'synchronicity' (meaningful coincidences) governs Jung's, where the events that occur in our lives are exactly those we need if we are to learn.

For Freud, the libido and sex-drive were all important to human motivation; for Jung it was one motivation among several.

For Freud, the unconscious were the repository of repressed emotions and desires. For Jung, in addition to a personal unconscious, humans also have a 'collective unconscious' connecting the individual to others in the past and present. The aim of life was the integration of the unconscious 'shadow' (parts of our nature that we tend to disown and feel bad about) with the personal conscious 'ego' to form a more rounded 'Self'. The 'Self' is in turn connected to and informed by the collective unconscious. Jung called this process of gradual transformation 'individuation'. Accordingly, personal and collective unconscious is brought into full awareness, thereby achieving inner harmony, maturation of personality and fullness of life.

---

[76] My thanks to Larry Culliford for his guidance on this section.

Freud concentrated on people with psychological problems identified as patients. His work was to make life for them less emotionally fraught and more manageable. His could be described as a mechanistic rather than an organic view of life.

Jung's objective was to help individuals – both people with problems and those who wanted somehow to grow and develop their personalities. His aims and methods encouraged penetration beneath the mask, the false 'persona' of the ego, going further than making lives manageable, working towards discovery of our true selves, our spiritual nature and the divine.

For Freud, optimism was an illusion, a groundless aspiration that humanity has developed in order to help us cope with life. For Jung, optimism, which can be viewed as arising from spiritual energy, was ubiquitous – should we choose to tap into it.

For Freud, life had no purpose beyond biological necessity, to keep reproducing ourselves as a species. For Jung, life had a divine purpose. For Freud there was no God. For Jung, there was only God.

We choose which guru we prefer. I am a confirmed Jungian. I declare an interest. Joanna was named after Anna Freud, Sigmund's daughter, who over two prolonged periods analysed a rather wonderful family member and helped make their life more manageable. But is making a life manageable enough? What about inner spiritual growth and reaching deep understanding?

Which thinker, Freud or Jung, chimes more with you, and why?

Alternative models of the human psyche

The mystical seventeenth-century poet John Donne (1572–1631) famously wrote, 'No man is an island entire of itself; every man / is a piece of the continent, a part of the main'.[77] His poetry is admired in the West but his words have made little impression on the way we live. Most people from the developed Western world see the individual as entirely separate. The dominant model of the human psyche suggests that we must construct a personal ego for ourselves, which has the maximisation of our own pleasure and minimisation of pain as the principal motive. Our minds are constantly looking into the future and back into the past in order to make life more manageable, rather than living in the present.

Many people believe that the ego and mental processes are all there is to life, and can see no place either for God or any ultimate meaning. Some get angry when their viewpoint is challenged, and deny any possibility of any truth outside rational human thought, as they see it. They see their own truth as the only truth.

If we allow ourselves to become more mindfully aware of the present moment, we recognise that the mind is bigger than we habitually imagine it to be. It is only when living in the present moment that we find we are not isolated islands but connected to the whole of humanity. If rigid

---

[77] Originally published 1624, a modern version can be found in Donne, J. (1975). *Devotions upon Emergent Occasions*. Oxford University Press.

thinkers, including militant atheists, were to spend a month in a monastery or Buddhist temple being silent while focusing their attention on the present moment, they might realise this. But silence, and the humility it requires, do not seem to appeal to them. You do not have to go to a monastery to discover stillness. It is here, now. It is in fact only here, now.

Many religious believers commit the same fallacy. They become egocentric about their own faith, believing that they have the monopoly on God's truth. They too need to live more in the present, to be less judgemental and to show more humility, and to connect with and deeply listen to the truths of people of other faiths, and none. Doing so will help them to recognise universal as opposed to partial truths. 'The only wisdom we can hope to acquire,' wrote T.S. Eliot in the *Four Quartets*, 'is the wisdom of humility'. He continued, 'humility is endless'.[78]

The diagram below portrays a series of oscillations.

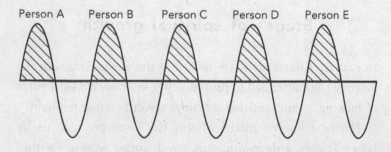

Person A   Person B   Person C   Person D   Person E

---

[78] Eliot, T.S. (1979). *Four Quartets* (1944). London and Boston: Faber and Faber.

The straight line represents the border between the conscious and unconscious mind, between our lives awake and our dreams. Most people inhabit the area above the line. They view others as entirely separate to themselves. If we expand our understanding of who we are, and bring our unconscious minds into conscious awareness, we will recognise that we are connected not only with each other but with the entire sentient universe.

All we have to do is become aware, minute by minute, of what is happening around us in the present moment – the sights, the sounds, the smells, the tastes, while at the same time become aware, non-judgementally, of everything that is happening inside our minds. This means, for example, that rather than getting annoyed by the ceaseless chatter of our thought processes, we learn to merely observe the chatter and let go of our frustration. The more we practise this, the more we will become integrated people, and the more we will move beyond happiness to joy.

Stages of spiritual growth

In Part III, Chapter One we looked at the eleven stages in the journey from utter hell to profound joy. We now consider ways of looking at our spiritual journeys towards enlightenment.

The best known model of this has been given to us by James Fowler, a developmental psychologist working within the theological tradition of Methodism,[79] who sees a seven-stage journey:

[79] Fowler, J. W. (1981). *Stages of Faith*, Harper & Row.

Stage	Title	Description
0	Primal or Undifferentiated	Learning about the safety of our environments, typically in the first couple of years of our lives, in order to develop the ability to trust.
1	Intuitive-Projective	Young children experience a fluidity of thought before they develop an ego restricting access to their subconscious.
2	Mythic-Literal	Schoolchildren typically have a strong belief in justice and meritocracy. They often misunderstand religions and stories and take them literally.
3	Synthetic-Conventional	Teenagers typically conform to known religious authorities as they develop their personal identity.
4	Individuative-Reflective	Young adults often struggle with faith, when they take responsibility for their feelings and beliefs. Becoming open-minded to the complexity of faith highlights contradictions.
5	Conjunctive	'Mid-life' adults learn to accept the paradoxes of faith and resolve the contradictions by transcending literal understanding.
6	Universalising	The wise individual embraces the universal principles of love and justice, treating everyone with compassion. They are often called 'enlightened'.

An alternative model of inner-growth is provided by Simon P. Walker,[80] a spiritual teacher I met ten years ago who has profoundly affected my life and that of many other teachers and leaders. He speaks with a clarity and simplicity born of his own experience. He is the best kind of ordained priest – humble, non-judgemental and compassionate.

I love his four-stage model of life:

Stage	Title	Description
1	Lack of awareness	Individuals live a compartmentalised life that is logical and detached; they are their own focus and are.defined by their achievements: they are unreflective and restless, preferring talking to listening.
2	Awareness	Individuals become curious and aware of discrepancies within themselves and their world-view; they seek personal growth; they become suspicious of dogma; they become more aware of their own inner-lives and take increasing responsibility for any failings.

[80]Walker, S.P. (2008). *The Leadership Community*. The Leadership Community.

3	Responsibility and choice	Individuals are honest, patient and disciplined; they listen before speaking and are generous with power and possessions; they are focused on the present and are comfortable when alone and with unresolved emotions; they seek to forgive and become increasingly aware of their journey.
4	Freedom	The trusting individual considers life a gift; they are content in all situations, learning, accepting and enjoying everything while needing nothing; they act from a deep place of love; they can accept power but do not need it; they are still and centred, always learning and can see beyond death.

Atheism v religion

Atheists have some very good reasons for rejecting religion. Terrible deeds have been done, and are being done today, in its name. Religion has often been a mask for a predominantly male elite who engage in the impoverishment of the masses on behalf of the powerful and articulate.

But we should not confuse religion with the existence of a spiritual realm, or God. One is the path (or not, as the case may be); the other is the destination. Many who follow religion reject reason. The approach I'm advocating here is to use reason and never to abandon it, to find the highest levels of fulfilment and our deepest meanings in life.

We may have many reasons for rejecting God and religion. Whether you are a believer or a committed atheist, take some time to explore either your doubts or your rationale for rejecting the spiritual realm. These are the biggest of life's big questions, so take your time. Even people of faith have arguments and disappointments with religion. On the right-hand side of the table, try to assess the objectivity of your criticisms and concerns.

	Doubts and reasons for rejecting either religion or God	Assessment of this critique or concern
1		
2		
3		
4		
5		

Religious fundamentalists have much in common with militant atheists.

- They believe that their own experience and insights are better than the insights of others.

- They consider that their understanding of science, philosophy or religion entitles them to claim a monopoly on truth.
- They reject as groundless the spiritual insights of some of the greatest artists, poets, thinkers and statesmen that the world has known.
- They frequently highlight the failings of practitioners of other beliefs, which they claim to be typical of all those who hold those beliefs.

They have intellectually coherent mastery of their own disciplines in the rational part of their minds, without having a holistic awareness of their entire minds, including their unconscious.

Opening up to joy

Over the remaining chapters of this book, five further paths are described to help us move beyond happiness to joy. We may well find that instead of feeling pushed, as we did on the journey to happiness, we will feel a *pull*, which could come from other people, a force beyond us or from our own innermost being.

- **INQUIRY** and self-discovery are essential if we are to become integrated and more fully ourselves. Only when we become whole and unified will we be able to experience joy. To achieve this, we need to learn detachment.
- **JOURNEYING** is essential if we are to find joy. We have to leave

the secure land of happiness, and leave our sure and trusted points of reference behind us to embark on a voyage into the unknown.

- **KARMA** explains how what we experience in life is the product of our past actions. We must learn to act with compassion and understanding towards all and to commit selfless actions if we are to erase the problems caused from our bad actions in the past. Forgiving others and ourselves is essential if we are to be forgiven for our wrongs.

- **LITURGY** is the core of worship and prayer, which many will need on their journey.

- **MEDITATION**, mindfulness and contemplation complete this five-part process. We need to become aware of the present moment and what is real, and leave behind what is unreal.

Some of us will be more drawn to one or two of these ways than the others. Or we may choose to pursue all five at the same time. The route is unimportant compared to the destination.

2.

Inquiry

Inquiry is the first of the paths towards the achievement of the deepest levels of joy. We inquire to discover what is true, to clear away myth and belief and to learn how to embrace the real. Through our inquiry we will discover our fullest selves, including the contents of our unconscious mind. We will learn how to live fully consciously in the present moment, as opposed to being asleep, or half asleep, lost in thoughts about the past.

If we want to go beyond happiness we have no alternative but to inquire into ourselves. As Socrates said, 'the unexamined life is not worth living'.[81] Yet many of us who are trapped in happiness and self-satisfaction don't seem to want to examine our lives in detail. We go through our lives a mystery unto ourselves.

Our unconscious minds, which govern so much of our motivation, thinking and feeling, we treat as unknown and, worse, unknowable. In Shakespeare's *King Lear*, Regan said

---

[81] Stokes, M.C. (1997). *Plato: Apology of Socrates.* Aris & Phillips.

of her father, Lear, 'he hath ever but slenderly known himself'.[82] In truth, most of us only slenderly know ourselves. We know what we know, and we arrogantly think that is all there is *to* know. Our conscious minds construct our egos, which prioritise reason and leave little or no space for ambiguity, compassion or spirituality. When we do know ourselves better, indeed know ourselves fully, we will realise the truth of the Islamic saying 'whoever knows himself, he knows his lord'.[83]

Casting light on our shadow

The shadow is nothing more nor less than the unconscious mind. Following Jung, we can say that the shadow includes both positive and negative elements that are ordinarily beyond the reach of our conscious minds. 'Everyone carries a shadow and the less it is embodied in the individual's conscious life, the blacker and denser it is.'[84]

The shadow is neither bad nor good, and we should not demonise it. Within it reside some of the most creative and deepest aspects of our being. To become fully whole, we need to embrace it. Our shadow is the depository of what we do not like to acknowledge about ourselves, so we are particularly

[82] Shakespeare, W. (2005). *The Tragedy of King Lear (Vol. 20)*. Cambridge University Press. Act I: Scene 1.

[83] Generally attributed to Ibn Arabi (1165–1240): Al'Arabi, I., (1980). *The Bezels of Wisdom*. (R. W. J. Austin, trans.) Mahwah, N.J.: Paulist Press.

[84] Jung, C.G. (2014). *Collected Works of C.G. Jung, Volume 11: Psychology and Religion: West and East*. Princeton University Press. p. 131.

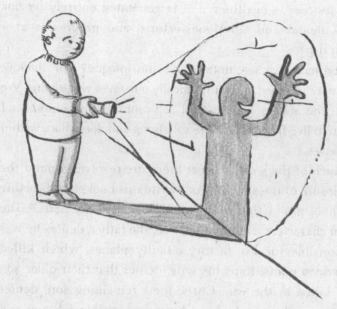

We inquire and discover what is true.

adept at seeing in others the very desires, impulses and attributes that we are denying in ourselves.

Assimilation of our shadow should be a gentle process if it is to be of lasting benefit. It needs time and should not be rushed. This is one of many reasons why illegal substances that claim to be 'mind-opening' are best avoided. The process is healthier if it is generated entirely by our own mental and emotional efforts, and progresses at a natural pace.

The more we see, understand and integrate our shadow, the more rounded and authentically ourselves we become. We leave the always restless and self-centred ego behind, and begin to live from a far more satisfying and deep place within ourselves.

Much of the world's great literature revolves around the disclosure of the shadow. As I write this book, I'm directing a school production of Arthur Miller's *All My Sons*.[85] The main characters live in denial. Joe, the father, denies he was responsible for his factory's faulty planes, which killed American pilots. Kate, his wife, denies that their older son was killed in the war. Chris, their remaining son, denies that the father could have been responsible for any evil action.

Their shadows are progressively lifted throughout the play, which culminates in Joe's recognition that the pilots who were killed by his greed were in fact, 'all my sons'. He goes off and puts a bullet in his head. Self-realisation can be risky if rushed. We need to move gently into the shining light.

---

[85] Miller, A. (1947). *All My Sons: Drama in Three Acts*. Penguin.

We walk around with a metaphorical tarpaulin draped over
our neck and shoulders.

We all walk around with a metaphorical tarpaulin draped over our head and shoulders. It weighs us down, prevents us from being the person we want to be and could be. Our tarpaulin has been formed from all the self-doubt and self-criticism that we have accumulated over our lives. To become the very best that we could be, we need to lighten and then cast off our tarpaulin altogether.

As always, it is easier to see others weighed down than to realise that we are too. Look out of the window and you will see people walking the streets weighed down by this invisible weight. This chapter will help you inquire about your own burden, and how you might lift it.

Modes of inquiry

Inquiry into our deeper natures and our shadow selves is not some dreary or anxiety-making work. On the contrary, like all discovery and research, it is deeply rewarding and fascinating. That's not to say that you won't be encountering some challenging thoughts. Entering into the inquiry in a positive spirit is vital.

Many of us choose to enlist the help of a guide. We might call that person a 'therapist' if they are helping us along the journey from '-5' to 'zero', a 'coach' if they are helping us move from 'zero' to '+3', and a 'spiritual counsellor' if they are taking us all the way to '+5'. We can call them whatever we like: in reality they are all operating on a continuum towards the realisation of our full potential and purpose.

Working in groups

'T-groups' or training groups (sometimes 'encounter' or human relations groups) spread from the 1940s as a way for the participants to gain insights into themselves based on the feedback of others. Many remarkable groups exist to help the exploration of spirituality and spiritual philosophy. For people who would like to investigate from a starting point within the Christian tradition, they include Julian meetings inspired by the writings of Julian of Norwich and Taizé groups, which look to the great spiritual and musical tradition of the Taizé monastic community in Burgundy in the east of France.[86] The range of these groups, religious, spiritual or humanist, is vast. Finding the right one may take time. I totally rejected the organised religion of school Anglicanism and it put me off religion for years. But in my twenties I encountered meditation, yoga and interfaith groups and found them profoundly meaningful and stimulating. The internet is full of ideas.

All of us have to choose which path to follow and some of us might conclude that making progress on our own is our preference. It might be easier than we had thought. Here are two ways of setting out.

Who am I?

Ramana Maharshi, whose luminous eyes appeared in Part III, Chapter One, advocated this particular form of self-inquiry.

---

[86] See http://www.taize.fr/en

For Maharshi, the ego or the 'I'-thought is ultimately unreal, a construct that dissolves upon deep inquiry. He saw the disappearance of the 'I' as the way to wisdom, arguing that the restless 'I' constantly stops us experiencing joy and truth. All that is required to eliminate the insubstantial ego is the persistent answering of the question, 'who am I?' We should be asking ourselves the question throughout the day in order to discover the illusory nature of the 'I'. Maharshi called God the 'Self' and saw it as the source of all awareness within us.

'The truth is that Self is constant and unintermittent awareness,' Maharshi said.[87] 'The object of inquiry is to find the true nature of the Self as awareness. Let us practise inquiry so long as separation is perceived.'

Maharshi's approach has been found helpful by many people. Ample guidance can be found about the practice in published books and on the internet. I have no doubt that he is one of the great sages of the last hundred and more years.

Investigating our own shadows

We can ignore our shadow and live purely from our conscious ego, hoping to keep our shadow buried deep away. Or we can choose to acknowledge it and shine a light on its entirety.

The ten questions below are designed to help illuminate our shadow. You might choose to work on them on your own or you might find it more helpful to work with others. As

[87]Godman, D., & Maharshi, S. (1991). *Be As You Are: The Teachings of Sri Ramana Maharshi*. Penguin UK.

long as they are prepared to tell you the truth, rather than what they think you want to hear about yourself, their comments will be invaluable. Working with people who are good for us provides support and balance. It is important to enjoy this journey, and laughing as we discover the absurdity of ourselves is always helpful.

Answering these ten questions fully may well take several weeks. Do not hurry to finish. Leave any which do not appeal to you. Remember that are you being asked to write down thoughts that are coming out of the unconscious mind, which is why the insights of others can be helpful, because they see us as we truly are rather than as actors presenting our acceptable or winning faces.

ACTIONS

List in the box below five actions you have previously taken, or which you are repeatedly taking, which are causing damage and hurt to others. On the right-hand side, list actions that are helpful to others, to provide balance.

	Actions that cause damage or hurt	Actions that are helpful
1		
2		
3		
4		
5		

Ask yourself why you took or are taking these actions. What is motivating you, and from where inside you is that action emanating? By understanding your hurtful behaviours better, you come closer to ceasing to commit them.

BELIEFS

It is important to realise the beliefs that you hold about yourself, other people or peoples, animals or organisations of which you are not proud. We suppress these, hence the need to probe any racist, sexist or homophobic thoughts. List them boldly, while balancing them with a list of positive beliefs.

	Beliefs of which you are not proud	Beliefs which are positive
1		
2		
3		
4		
5		

By writing down these beliefs, you are coming closer to letting go of their grip on you. Unacknowledged prejudice is dangerous. Place these unwelcome beliefs in the forefront of your mind, probe and analyse them and ask whether you still want to be attached to them.

FANTASIES

What have been your repeating fantasies, perhaps from childhood, those which regularly float into your mind? Sexual fantasies may occur to you first, but there will be many others. Clues may come from scenes from books, films or plays that appeal to you strongly for reasons that you may not always understand. On the right-hand side of the table, list fantasies that you characterise as positive and helpful.

	Repeating fantasies	Positive fantasies
1		
2		
3		
4		
5		

Ask yourself what it is about these fantasies that makes them so important to you. Bring them fully into your conscious mind, however absurd, embarrassing or painful they may be. My own revolve principally around my saving people in danger, or being collected (from where?) by a warm and loving woman. Your own fantasies will tell you much about your shadow.

In our forties, Joanna and I started seeing a family therapist to help us understand each other better. She was kind but mechanical and I yearned for her to ask what really mattered to us, even what books or films really excited us. For me at the time, it was a film of a book by Nevil Shute called *No Highway*, which featured an eccentric scientist played by Jimmy Stewart. He was persistently rejected by women but at the end of the film a glamorous female turned up to look after him. She was the figure I yearned to find. She was already in my life, Joanna. I had yet fully to realise it.

FEARS

What are your worst fears, either those you have managed to overcome or which still plague you? Listing them probably won't be a comfortable experience but you may find it helpful. In the right-hand column, note any occasions when you faced these fears, when you have been at your bravest. Ask yourself what it took to confront the fears.

	Worst fears	Occasions when you faced them
1		
2		

3	
4	
5	

Your fears of loss, abandonment, anonymity or extinction have all occurred for a reason. Remember, every single fear, even the most seemingly intractable, can be lifted and disappear. Cognitive behavioural therapy can be a great source of help. We come to realise the irrationality of our fear, we understand that it exists for a reason and present-minded awareness is used to help our growth in understanding it. Believe that you can overcome your fears and you will be able to do so. Fears are only as strong as we let them be. With freedom from fear, comes joy.

HATES

From whom or what do you recoil? Investigate your hates and intense dislikes, making as full a list as possible, including states of mind and abstract ideas as well as the concrete. In the right-hand column of the table overleaf, list the people, the organisations and the ideas that you most love.

	Hates	Loves
1		
2		
3		
4		
5		

Ask yourself why you hate. Hatred always enslaves, belittles and demeans us – so why do we damage ourselves by allowing it any part in our lives? Examine deeply the genesis and nature of your hates. How far are they reflections of what you don't like about yourself? What changes when/if you have compassion towards those you think have wronged you? How does it feel if you forgive, and where is the resistance to that notion of forgiveness coming from?

HOPES

What are your deepest hopes for your own life, including those for your family, friends and organisations? You are not being asked here to fill in an annual development plan. You are to fill in a *life-long* plan, and your budget is unlimited. There is no right-hand column in this box. List your hopes even if you believe they are neither aspirational nor admirable.

Deepest hopes
1
2
3
4
5

What are these deepest aspirations saying about you? What is their source and motivation? Are they emanating from a desire to fulfil your own dreams, or those you have either taken on from other people or are projecting on to others? Are you seeking to make your aspirations their aspirations?

INFLUENCES

Who or what has influenced you for the worse in your life? Return to the thoughts, ideas, people and possessions that have pointed you away from joy, which degrade you and fill you with a sense of shame? In the right-hand column, list those that lift you up.

Negative influences	Positive influences
1	
2	

3	
4	
5	

Why are you continuing to let yourself be influenced by those people or thoughts you know are harmful to you? Who is in charge of that choice? What will it take to push you towards being influenced only positively, and ending your attachment to negative influences?

PRESSURES

What are the pressures that drive you, the things you feel you *ought* to be doing? If you struggle to think of any, look for obligations that are making you unhappy. Be specific about them, for example, to make money, partner a certain kind of person or to belittle certain people or causes when you are in public.

	Pressures
1	
2	
3	
4	
5	

It is important to be extraordinarily honest about the pressures placed upon you. Ask yourself whether they really are unavoidable or whether you have discretion over them. If they are unwelcome, what will you do to release their hold? Bringing them into your conscious awareness will help release them, by making you aware that you have choices.

PRIDE

Turn your thinking to occasions when you have felt humiliated. Who humiliated you and how did you respond? Be honest, even if your response was uncontrollable rage. Explore what it is that felt undermined, vulnerable and exposed because of what happened. It will give you a powerful insight about a mismatch between your conscious self-image and your unconscious. Identifying what makes us feel humiliated is a door into our unconscious.

	Humiliating occasions	Which aspect of you felt undermined
1		
2		
3		
4		

5

Having identified the humiliation, try to observe humiliating occasions in action, pulling back from your habitual response and reacting with more equanimity. Is it really worth becoming humiliated: why do that to yourself? Admitting to weaknesses is profoundly liberating and dispels your aura of invincibility, which repels rather than attracts others to you.

TRAITS

What are the character traits of which you are least proud, and which you find hardest to admit to yourself as well as to others? The very act of naming these will be helpful. In the right-hand column, list those traits of which you are most proud.

	Traits of which you are least proud	Traits of which you are most proud
1		
2		
3		
4		
5		

Identification requires honesty but once you have named and 'owned' your unattractive traits, you will be well on the path to releasing their hold on you. The shadow loves the dark; shedding light on it dismantles its potency.

So, is that it? Does being honest about our shadow mean that we are now in harmony with our full selves? Well, of course there is always further to go, but the very act of acknowledging our shadow is the first step to integrating it and making us whole. Embracing our shadow makes us less judgemental, more compassionate, less unsteady, more considered. We will start to experience the bliss of accepting ourselves, others and the world as we and they are. Recognising that we have little or no power to change anything other than ourselves puts us firmly on the path to wisdom and joy.

The more profoundly you are able to inquire, the more fully you are able to accept yourself and the more you loosen your attachment to ideas you hold about yourself and others, the more you will experience joy. Inquiry might take you all the way: it will certainly take you some of the way. For most people though, it will also be necessary to go on a journey . . .

3.

Journey

We spend our lives going on journeys to faraway places, virtually or in reality, but many of us don't seem to travel far. We go away with our endlessly chattering mind, which prevents us from deeply engaging with the peoples and places we visit. We can travel 10,000 miles but not travel an inch.

This chapter is about a different kind of journey. An inner journey. The aim is not to see, photograph and try to possess part of the world: the aim is to travel inside and also beyond ourselves and our current self-limitations. And by doing that, we come to see the world afresh, as it really is.

When did you last spend time on your own, without your job, family or the company of friends to distract you? Unless we allow ourselves regular periods of being utterly alone and sitting in silence, we will not discover who we are. Without undertaking a journey that will bring us home transformed, we will not discover joy. If we are travelling in the right direction and at the right speed, we will feel an inner excitement, an anticipation. But come off that path and we experience pain of rising intensity until we recognise we have no alternative but to re-join the path. T.S. Eliot's words from the *Four Quartets* encapsulate the whole spirit of the journey, and why it is necessary. 'And the end of all our exploring / Will be to arrive where we started / And know the place for the first time.'[88] How can we arrive there? Will we know it?

Discovering your purpose

I believe we all have a duty to find our purpose in life. We were born to fulfil that purpose, and we were given free will to make choices so that we can achieve it. As we grow older, we will be at different stages along the path towards it. Franciscan writer Richard Rohr speaks of the 'two halves of life'.[89] In the first half we are builders – of our qualifications, families and careers. In the second half we let it all go – our ego-centred preoccupations, our attachment to possessions and status. Our self-importance and pride evaporates. We find our lives governed by a less assertive and more compassionate centre within us.

Some people move into the second half as early as their thirties. More usually, it occurs in our fifties or sixties. Some never achieve it and go to their graves still trumpeting their achievements and with their restless egos defending their possessions and reputations even as the light fades that one final time.

---

[88] Eliot, T.S. (1979). *Four Quartets* (1944). London and Boston: Faber and Faber.
[89] Rohr, R. (2011). *Falling Upward: A Spirituality for the Two Halves of Life.* John Wiley & Sons.

How would you describe your own purpose on earth? This is a question that we posed at the beginning of the book. It's time to ask it again, in the hope that the work you've undertaken over the course of reading will allow you to answer it more fluently, honestly and fully. Look forward to that last day alive, when you know that you will shortly die, and imagine that you can clearly see what your own unique mission was. In the box below, describe it, in as much detail as you can manage.

My life's mission

Now, in this smaller box, evaluate the progress you have made towards it.

Progress towards my mission

What has prevented you from moving further along that path already? What has knocked you off your path when you lost your way? Write about those obstacles in the left-hand column, and how you plan to overcome them on the right. Remember, misfortune may be just what we need to get us on our path.

Obstacles	How to overcome them

Incorporating pilgrimage into our journey

The experience of physical journeying to places of special spiritual significance is common in all belief systems. Pilgrims are cleansed and gain spiritual insights as a result. Hindus are encouraged to undertake pilgrimages to sites such as the River Ganges, or to see revered gurus. For Muslims, the journey to Mecca is one of the five pillars of their faith, to be attempted at least once in everyone's life. Muslims also visit Medina, the second holiest place in Islam, and Jerusalem, the third holiest. For early Christians, visiting the sites of the life of Jesus was considered important. Pilgrimage to places associated with saints, martyrs, apostles and apparitions became popular in later centuries. One of the most celebrated Christian pilgrimages is the visit, along the Way of Saint James, to Santiago de Compostela in northern Spain. Undertaking a pilgrimage is often an experience of profound spiritual significance for the pilgrim: the greater the degree of difficulty, the richer and deeper the reward.

But to experience the full richness of inner joy, we may need to tailor our own, solitary journey. It may not be to a holy site at all, unless by 'a holy site', we mean our innermost soul.

The supreme value of spending time alone with ourselves, without the distractions of the world and without the trappings of personal wealth, power and prestige, is that it allows us to confront ourselves as we are. It may be that you too will find this by going on a pilgrimage. Perhaps you would benefit from spending time on a retreat, whether it is Christian or Buddhist, or organised by other faiths or by bodies with no specific affiliation. You may simply want to take a trip to somewhere you know you will experience deep solitude and peace.

Explore your thoughts about going on a pilgrimage or a retreat. Do some research to discover one that you think will suit you. Make a commitment and do it. It is never too late.

Thoughts about going on a pilgrimage or retreat

In the box below, write a plan for how you will spend such time on your own.

> Plan for spending time alone
>
>
>
>
>
>

'Here is my journey's end,'[90] says Othello in Act V of Shakespeare's great tragedy. Yet Othello has reached less self-knowledge than many of Shakespeare's tragic heroes. He has been unable to overcome the dark forces of jealousy in his unconscious mind, and ends up killing the wife he loves so dearly.

We all have journeys to make, whether or not we acknowledge them. Not all of them end well, especially when we ignore the calling to embark.

---

[90] Shakespeare, W. (1903). *The Tragedy of Othello*. Methuen.

What will it cost?

The ostensible goal of our journeys will vary from person to person but all journeys require one particular ending: we need to let go of our attachments. The person who possesses everything in the world and is profoundly attached to those riches and status, to their idea of themselves, has nothing. The person who may or may not have wealth and status, but has no attachment to them, possesses everything.

No one has better encapsulated this dichotomy than T.S. Eliot when he wrote that our journey is to 'a condition of complete simplicity (costing not less than everything).'[91] Our journey will end when we have given up our ego, with all its frantic attachments, and we live from our deepest soul, which through possessing nothing is in communion with everything.

[91] Eliot, T.S. (1979). *Four Quartets* (1944). London and Boston: Faber and Faber.

4.

Karma

You might be thinking that karma is an alien idea of little
pertinence to your life. It's true that most people in the West
have ignored or misunderstood the concept, to the detriment
of our spiritual growth. Karma speaks not only of the impact
of our thoughts and deeds but also to the way they come back
to us.

Despite the underlying assumption most of us live by, which
is that we are isolated entities in the universe, I am convinced
we are all interconnected in the most profoundly complex
and subtle ways. Everything we think and do sends ripples
far and wide, which sooner or later hit a distant wall and
rebound to us. Our good actions result in happiness and joy:
bad actions return to us in the form of unhappiness and
misery. No escape is possible. No goodness, no joy. Badness
lives.

The world's religions differ in many vital aspects. They are
united by an adherence to the 'golden rule', which can be
summarised as 'do unto others as you would have done unto

Everything we do sends ripples far and wide, that will come
back and revisit us.

yourself', or 'love others as you yourself would want to be loved.'[92]

Eastern religions emphasise reincarnation, the idea that we will keep returning to earth in some form until we become enlightened and act with loving kindness to all. Followers of reincarnation believe that those people who suffer physical, mental and material misfortune in this world have brought it upon themselves as a result of past actions. Christianity, Judaism and Islam, in contrast, emphasise that we have just one chance in life, and that a life of sin will lead to pain in the afterlife.

The debate about reincarnation, heaven and hell need not detain us here. Others may know the truth of these matters: I do not. But karma applies as much to us in the West as to those in the East.

On responsibility

The following propositions are clear: we are all responsible for our actions, and to deny responsibility does not excuse them. Kind and good actions make us happy, while bad actions lead to mental confusion and unhappiness. What greets us each day might appear random but is in fact exactly what we need to help us to choose how to act rightly, i.e. with wisdom and compassion. The difficulties that we experience in life will, to a significant extent, be the result of our wrong actions

---

[92] Armstrong, K. (2011). *Twelve Steps to a Compassionate Life*. Random House.

in the past. Where we have done wrong we should make amends, for the sake of others, but also for ourselves. While we are weighed down with sin, or bad actions from which we have not yet been released, we will never experience joy.

A hurt audit

However painful it may be, it is important to acknowledge the harm that we have done to others. The Alcoholics Anonymous twelve-step programme includes the determination to make amends with those we have hurt, and it is in the list for very good reason.

It's time to conduct an audit of those we have damaged. Distinguish on the left and right-hand sides of the table overleaf between those hurts we have inflicted that have been deliberate acts of will and those where others were hurt because of our selfishness or lack of compassion, albeit without any premeditated intention. You will need to probe your life with great honesty and candour, and the advice of loved ones may well be necessary for you to admit the full truth. The deeper the hurt that we have done to others, the harder it may be for us to even admit to it.

This list will not form up immediately. Take time over it and keep coming back and adding fresh material. You may want to refer to the hurt you have caused people in your family, friends and lovers, those at work and perhaps those you have barely known. Remember, every single act we have performed has consequences.

Turn your attention to the column on the right. It is where

we caused hurt intentionally that we need to make amends. We may have drunk too much, or were otherwise not in full control of our faculties. That is not an excuse. The very act of compiling this list honestly will itself be healing.

	Hurt caused accidentally	Hurt caused intentionally
1		
2		
3		
4		
5		

Writing down what has happened has taken us some way to the solution. Now set out in the following box how you plan to make amends to five people or causes that you have consciously hurt by your actions.

You must be prepared for rebuff. It may well be that those you have injured are not ready, or do not want to accept your overtures. If your desire to make amends is totally sincere, and you are full of humility and genuine sorrow, your entreaty is more likely to be accepted.

Those you have hurt may no longer be alive, and causes that you damaged may have withered and died. You can still make your peace with those who passed away, or with their families, or you can support causes similar to the one that has disappeared. Doing this sincerely will lift a real weight from your shoulders. Some of the karmic damage within you will be dissolved.

Means to make amends
1
2
3
4
5

Selfless giving

Selfless giving unrelated to those you have hurt is another way of addressing your karmic deficit. Pursuing good deeds, without any motive of personal gain, will steadily lighten your load. It is better if no one knows of these actions, because if you are seeking their approval or good opinion then your actions are no longer motiveless.

As you go through each day, examine your 'karmic footprint'. From the moment you wake to the moment you go to sleep, are you making the burdens of others lighter or heavier? It is not only what you do, but what you think. Our thinking leads to our actions, our actions to our habits, our habits to our character.

Make a list of some of your habitual actions that are genuinely selfless. It might be helping somebody out on your journey to work. It could be avoiding using towels unnecessarily, filling our plates with far more food than we need, and leaving rooms tidy. It could be picking up rubbish when you are out and about and depositing it in bins, or recycling your own waste.

Selfless habitual actions
1
2
3
4
5

Volunteering is an excellent example of selfless service. We could all be volunteering regularly, at least several times a year. The further the activity takes you outside your comfort zone, for example helping in an overnight shelter for the homeless, the more benefit you will receive and the more your own deficit of bad deeds will be erased. You may want to give blood or plan to donate vital organs when you die. We are all part of something much bigger than our little egos can ever conceive: volunteering reminds us that we belong.

Sacred space and footprint

A novel way to address the impact of our actions is to use a conscious mental device to make visible our invisible self. Jesus teaches this when he says, 'Forgive us our trespasses, as we forgive those who trespass against us.'[93] 'Trespass' here is a mental device making visible the footprint we leave upon others in the world, moment by moment, through our words, actions and intents.

Noticing our own footprint leads us to tread more lightly, be conscious of others' boundaries and treat another's self as sacred space. Children are now learning such self-inquiry at a young age through the 'Footprints Programme for Schools'.[94] By such practice we can also start to cast light on the impact of our presence in the world.

Agape and compassion

Agape, or selfless love, is the natural expression of all who are on the highest spiritual path and is the natural state of all who are in the highest phase of evolution.

The writer and former nun, Karen Armstrong, argues that

---

[93] Matthew 6.5–15. King James Version.
[94] See http://www.footprintsschoolsprogramme.co.uk

compassion lies at the heart of all great religions as well as many non-religious systems of thought.[95] Compassion allows human beings to overcome what she calls the 'four Fs' that motivate those of us who have not risen above the most basic level, i.e. feeding, fighting, fleeing and 'for want of a more basic word', as she puts it, reproduction. This 'old brain' thinking was bequeathed to us by reptiles many million years ago, yet the obsession with personal survival and gain is still prevalent in many people today. Our 'new brain', the neocortex, is the seat of reasoning and allows for a higher order and less ego-centred form of thinking.

Armstrong gives prominence to the term coined by German philosopher Karl Jaspers, 'the Axial Age'; the period 800–200 BC when a spiritual awakening occurred, including Confucianism, Buddhism and the rise of Platonism. Selfless love was a common quality advocated by these pre-Christian systems. Christianity did not invent the concept: Jesus highlighted its sovereign importance.

The other three forms of love described by C.S. Lewis – love of family, love of friends and sexual love – are all to a degree self-centred. *Agape* alone yields no benefit or consolation to the ego beyond knowing that we are doing good. *Agape* is the sovereign path to joy.

List five ways that you will commit to leading a life where agape becomes not the exception but the norm.

---

[95] Armstrong, K. (2011). *Twelve Steps to a Compassionate Life.* Random House.

Ways to commit to agape
1
2
3
4
5

Joanna has just walked into our bedroom, where I have secluded myself to work on this book. I am distantly aware of the energetic flapping of fresh linen from the vicinity of the bed. 'What are you doing?' she asks. 'Correcting a passage from the happiness book,' I respond. 'Which section?' she asks, slightly breathless from her exertions. 'Selfless love.' 'Typical. Why don't you put some into practice?' she mutters, as she disappears out of the bedroom, used bedclothes scrunched in hand. We could all of us stand to introduce a little more agape into our lives.

5.

Liturgy

What of prayer? For many spiritual aspirants it lies at the heart of their practice. It has not been forgotten here but I think its place does need to be investigated.

The previous three chapters discussed inquiring into who we are, making a journey to discover our unique destination in life and the carrying out of good deeds while making amends to those we have hurt. Each and all of these will take us on the path of greater joy.

So too will the fourth path, which is the following of a liturgy. The term is derived from the Greek word *leitourgia*, formed of two words, *leitos* (public) and *ergon* (work), literally meaning work of the people. Liturgy is thus corporate worship. A liturgy is followed by all the world's religions. They have many common forms, typically prayers, religious songs, readings from holy texts and some form of sermon or homily.

Liturgies are often tightly controlled by religious authorities, which arrogate to themselves the power of determining which form of religious service is authentic, which erroneous. At one end of the spectrum are highly formulaic and rigid services, following a very precise pattern: at the other, a much freer form of service. Within Christianity, we might place Roman Catholicism at one end and Quakerism at the other. Common to all liturgies, though, is prayer, which is of three main kinds: gratitude, devotion and supplication. Some people are more drawn to one form of prayer than others.

Prayer as gratitude

We have seen how expressing gratitude is important to finding happiness. Those who regularly do so are better connected to others and lead more rewarding and fulfilled lives.

If we are to move beyond happiness we need to be grateful not just for individual events when they go well, but to cultivate an attitude of deep appreciation for *everything* that we have in life, including what we do not like. Since developing cancer in 2011, Joanna has found fresh depth and meaning in her Jewish faith. Judaism is full of expressions of gratitude. At the start of each day she says 'Modah Ani'. These words express her gratitude for being kept alive and brought to the day which is just about to begin.

Imagine if we were to be constantly giving thanks, even for the times that we do not like. One change would be a gradual easing of the pain we experience from what we choose to label 'bad'.

List overleaf five regular factors in your life that you most definitely do not enjoy or like. They might be events, people or emotions. On the right-hand side of the table, write some words of praise expressing appreciation for them.

	Factor you do not enjoy or like	Praise and appreciation
1		
2		
3		
4		
5		

What is being suggested here is that we become constantly grateful for what we have. Not just for the food we eat, pleasant or otherwise, but for fresh air, for shelter, for clean water, for loving homes, families, friends and jobs, if we have them. Having the prayer of thanks in our mind will allow us to be much better connected with the world, to find energy and appreciation and to be much more fully alive.

'Pray without ceasing' advises Paul in his fifth letter to the Thessalonians.[96] My experience is that when I am mindfully present there is always the thought of prayer. *The Jesus Prayer*, 'Lord Jesus Christ, son of God, have mercy on me,'[97] or the

---

[96] Thessalonians. 5:16–18. King James Version.

[97] Barrington-Ward, S. (2007). *The Jesus Prayer*. Bible Reading Fellowship.

Lord's Prayer, are two that always come to mind. I try to start and finish the day with a prayer, and will often repeat prayers when going about my day's business.

It is all well and good to be grateful when life goes well, but is it possible to be grateful in the face of tragedy and disaster? No tragedy on earth eclipses in horror the Holocaust of the Second World War, although the decades are punctuated with many episodes of similar inhumanity and cruelty to smaller groups. Etty Hillesum[98] was a little known figure who perished in Auschwitz at the end of 1943, aged twenty-nine. For me, she ranks alongside the better known Dietrich Bonhoeffer and Martin Niemöller. She is my absolute heroine of the twentieth century.

When the Nazis invaded Holland she refused to flee, believing it was her duty to stay and to embrace the reality that she saw before her. During the course of 1941, with the Nazi net closing in on her and her family, she was deeply consoled by prayer, meditation and spirituality. Her mindful sense of the present moment allows her in her diary[99] to see and describe nature in all its beauty, even amid the most terrible suffering. Her awareness of God gave her an extraordinary power to fortify and give heart to all those terrified souls around her.

In September 1943 she was deported from Westerbork, the transit camp where Anne Frank and her family were temporarily incarcerated, to the concentration camps in the east. She threw a final postcard to a friend from the train,

---

[98] Culliford, L. (2011). *The Psychology of Spirituality: An Introduction.* Jessica Kingsley Publishers, pp. 181–190.

[99] Hillesum, E. (1999). *An Interrupted Life: The Diaries of Etty Hillesum* (A. Pomerans, trans.) Persephone Books.

which was later discovered. It describes how she and her party left the camp singing and how her heart was full of praise. She survived in Auschwitz for a few weeks before she was killed. Her ability to find joy in the face of the horror marks her out as one of the outstanding souls of the century.

Pope Benedict XVI said of her in his first audience after his resignation, 'This frail . . . young woman transfigured by faith, became a woman full of love and inner peace who was able to declare, "I live in constant intimacy with God."'[100]

Prayer as devotion

Devotion can be dangerous; we need to be extremely cautious when we devote our life to someone or something. Uncritical and undivided love is not always well directed.

We are all devoted to *something* in life. It might be our possessions, our career, our families, our animals, our team or even our self. We may become devoted to people who have particular gifts – singers, charismatic leaders or sporting stars. Such devotions will not take us far down the path to joy. They are all forms of self-love, beginning and ending with the ego. Fundamentalists who kill and maim because of devotion to their faith betray their faiths. They are high on themselves, in love with their glory in this life or the afterlife.

Only devotion to the infinite, the source of all love, peace

---

[100]Benedict XVI (13 February 2013) General Audience, *Paul VI Audience Hall*. Retrieved 14 November 2014 from http://vatican.va/holy_father/benedict_ xvi/audiences/2013/documents/hf_ben-xvii_aud_20130213_en.html

and wisdom is worthy. Such devotion will never cause harm to any being. Nor will it ensnare, entrap or limit us. It will never make us pick up arms against our fellow human beings. It will never cause us to increase our attachments; rather, it will loosen our attachment to all things of the world.

The idea of devotion in a spiritual context may be hard for some of us to grasp. Many of us lavish that care on our families, friends, our possessions or ourselves. But devotion to God? A step too far. It is instructive to try to be open-minded about this resistance. Where does it come from? Maybe we are angry because of some deep sadness in our life. We may not believe in God but we are nevertheless furious at God for letting us down and allowing us to suffer.

Use the box below to explore the obstacles that you have to the idea of devotion to an absolute being, and to expressing that undivided love with your whole heart. The very act of thinking through the blockages will help you along the path to expressing a devotion that we could all share.

Obstacles to devotion
1
2
3
4
5

Prayer as supplication

The third and final type of prayer asks God for something to happen, or not to happen, or to happen differently. This type of prayer is particularly vulnerable to being misused and misunderstood. If we don't like the answer (or lack of answer) to our prayer, we can become disillusioned.

Research studies conducted into the efficacy of praying for others provide uneven evidence of any benefit to, for example, sick patients who are on the receiving end of intense prayer. This research misunderstands the purpose of prayer as supplication. It isn't to change the outcome, although that can happen. Rather, it is to change *ourselves*, and the way in which we respond in the face of adversity.

Perhaps worldly adversity, even death, isn't as big a deal as it's cracked up to be. Imagine facing our own death and the death of those we love dearly, with equanimity. This is the ultimate liberation in life, because the fear of death, whether we acknowledge it or not, haunts us all. Yet if we can pray with complete conviction, it may be that the fear begins to loosen its hold. After all, if there is a God then death is not the end, even if our minds can never know that for certain.

Joanna's illness has forced us to think about her passing, as well as my own. I hold her hand in hospital and I tell her that I know that death is not the end. Nowhere on earth do I feel a greater sense of certainty than in the cemeteries of the First World War, which I have visited fifty and more times, taking groups of schoolchildren and adults. The silence of the graves draws you in and it is a place of utter peace, not terror.

In *Journey's End*, the play about that war by R.C. Sherriff, the hero – Captain Stanhope – reflects on his many friends who have died. In words that always touch me to the core, he says that death cannot be so lonely with so many who have gone there before. He adds with a pitiful poignancy, 'Sometimes, I think it's lonelier here.'[101]

It's time to revisit our exploration of our fears. List below some of your own greatest fears and anxieties about yourself or those you love, or about events that might happen. On the right-hand side, consider how your understanding of these events might be transformed through prayer, even if they cannot be changed.

	Greatest fears and anxieties	How to transform your understanding of them
1		
2		
3		
4		
5		

---

[101] Sherriff, R.C. (1929). *Journey's End: A Play*. Gollancz.

Ultimately, we cannot understand prayer rationally. Prayer takes us into a realm of mystery. *The Cloud of Unknowing*[102] is an anonymous work of Christian mystical prayer from the fourteenth century. The book suggests that only by abandoning all our beliefs and ideas about God and surrendering our minds and feelings to 'unknowingness', can we begin to comprehend the realm of God.

Sermons

Sermons are a core part of liturgy. Significant strength can be drawn from reading sermons and listening to today's great preachers in person or on YouTube.

Some of the most powerful preachers in the Christian tradition are St Paul, Charles Haddon Spurgeon, John Wesley and John Wycliffe. From the last century, Martin Luther King and the poet-preacher R.S. Thomas are among many we might benefit from listening to. Judaism and Islam have rich traditions of powerful and moving sermons, as have Eastern religions. We can learn from all great preachers, whatever our faith.

For me, the greatest sermon of all is the Sermon on the Mount.[103] It describes the utter truth of the human condition and speaks equally to those of all faith traditions. Many people have drawn inspiration from the *Desiderata*[104] (written in 1927 but which only became popular in the 1970s).

---

[102] Walsh, J. (Ed.). (1981). *The Cloud of Unknowing*. Paulist Press.

[103] Matthew. 5–7. King James Version.

[104] Ehrmann, M. (1995). *Desiderata: A Poem for a Way of Life*. Crown Publishers.

Religious songs and holy text

Almost all religions have music at their heart. The act of collective singing can bind believers together and elevate their spirit. Nothing can substitute for the experience of being present with other worshippers but much comfort and inspiration can be derived from listening to recordings of spiritual music.

Make a note below of your favourite spiritual music and try to spend some time listening to it. If you are not familiar with any, I urge you to investigate. It's powerfully moving stuff, even if you are not a believer.

Favourite spiritual music
1
2
3
4
5

My own favourite music includes Gregorian chants, Fauré's Requiem, Taizé music, Jewish spiritual songs and much Sufi singing. I first experienced a spiritual awakening when taking part in a satsang, a singing of Hindu songs after yoga, in the early 1980s. I loved then, as I love now, immersing myself in the powerfully repetitive and harmonious singing. I long ago lost any self-consciousness about being a public school headmaster (or biographer of Prime Ministers) in the midst of such a counter-cultural place. Yes, that is me standing up in assembly and telling the students to work harder. But it is also me immersed in prayer or singing Hindu songs, surrounded by people with cymbals, drums, beads and orange flowing garments. In the midst of all the music and the movement, the incense and the religious ecstasy, is total stillness.

We tend to read only religious texts from our own background. Much wisdom can be drawn from reading the sacred texts of other faiths. How can we possibly deny the validity of the faith of others when we know nothing about it? Reading with an open mind and heart will make us much less judgemental and damning.

The trap of liturgy

Liturgy can so easily become turgid. It is more likely to do so when it is seen as the end of the journey, rather than a signpost on the way.

Liturgy becomes a trap when religious officialdom tries to impose a rigid model on others, which might be meaningful or advantageous to the officials themselves but offers little to the mass of congregations. One reason why religions the world over lose supporters is because liturgy is so inert. The faithful sit passively and there is little active engagement of their hearts, minds or souls.

To be engaged, we need to be fully alive, and to be fully alive we need to be present. How to achieve this is discussed in the next chapter.

6

Meditation

Meditation, mindfulness and contemplation are suddenly everywhere. We could be forgiven for thinking that they are new devices, the latest fashion, and, as with all fashions, doomed to fade sooner or later. Nothing could be further from the truth. They are ancient practices and fundamental both to the world's religions and to a contemporary understanding of spirituality. The aim of all these processes is a quiet mind, one which is alert and completely focused on the present moment rather than constantly darting off in all directions with no conscious control. This still and receptive mind is attainable for all of us. Indeed, it is the ultimate aim for all of us. Such a mind is constantly joyful.

Mindfulness

Mindfulness is derived from Buddhist practice and is now prevalent in the West. I've referred to it many times throughout the book as it is a cornerstone of the way I understand my own journey to joy. To recap, mindfulness is the non-judge-mental awareness of our thoughts, emotions and sensations as they occur, moment to moment. Its primary uses are as a secular psychological aid to relaxation, and the amelioration of some chronic mental conditions including depression. Jon Kabat-Zinn was a key figure in its development as a treatment for a variety of mental and physical problems. In 1979 he founded the Mindfulness-Based Stress Reduction (MBSR) program at the University of Massachusetts.

By being encouraged to concentrate on present moment sensations in the body, particularly on the inhalation and exhalation of breath, practitioners become aware of a sense of inner calm and completeness. They develop an alternative awareness, which is separate from the feelings of depression or anxiety which so cloud their minds. Successive clinical studies have shown the mental health and physical benefits of mindfulness. Some research shows it to be more effective in tackling depression, and longer lasting in its impact, than medication or talking therapies.

The Mindfulness in Schools project has had remarkable success in Britain since its founding in 2011. It advocates a practice called .b (dot-be), where students as well as teachers are encouraged to 'stop, breathe and be': stop whatever they're doing, breathe in and out and simply notice the thoughts and feelings that arise without (if possible) identifying with them. FOFBOC is another of the recommended practices, standing for 'feet on floor, bums on chair'. It is an arresting way of reminding practitioners of the value simply of being rather than doing.

Helping the young to learn to self-calm is immensely

valuable. It gives them a tool they can use all their lives. Classes that begin with stillness allow students to let go of what happened in previous lessons or activities and to come fully into the moment to enjoy the experience that is about to begin. Adults can benefit, too. I begin every staff meeting with two minutes of stillness to allow all those present to collect themselves, let go of whatever thoughts or emotions are still circulating from what they were doing before and allow them to come more fully into the present moment.

It is better to practise mindfulness than to read about it. So find a chair now and sit still. With your back straight and your feet on the ground, inhale and exhale deeply, counting three beats to the inhalation and five to the exhalation. Use your full lung capacity; let go of tension in the belly and allow it to rise and fall. Notice the feelings and the thoughts that are circulating, but try not to comment on those thoughts and feelings. Merely see them arise and fade away, as feelings and thoughts always do.

Write down below the opportunities you have each day for mindful moments. You may find such occasions easier at the start of activities – sitting at the computer, before a journey or cooking dinner.

Opportunities to practise or lead mindfulness
1
2
3

4

5

Meditation

Mindfulness is typically regarded as a secular tool, yet the longer we practise it and experience even deeper levels of stillness, the more we realise its spiritual power. The part of you that is aware of the movement of thought and feeling is none other than your soul or *atman*, to use the Hindu term. The constantly restless mind that we are recognising and then learning to become detached from is the ego. Mindfulness is a journey from ego to soul.

Meditation, in contrast, is more unashamedly spiritual. The Latin word from which it is derived *meditari* means 'to think' or 'contemplate'. The Tibetan word for meditation, *gom,* means 'to become familiar with our soul'. Meditation is associated with the Eastern religions of Hinduism, Buddhism and Taoism but it is also strongly present in Judaism and Christianity and the Sufi tradition in Islam.

In Judaism, the ascetic tradition utilises meditation and the repetition of holy words; Karaite and Hasidic Judaism focus on the reading of religious texts and the development of mystical understanding of what is being conveyed. In Islam, the practice of Sufism sees practitioners using breath control and the repetition of holy words.

Christian meditation tends not to involve the repetition of words or concentration on any keyword, nor does it advocate the adoption of specific postures. Instead practitioners focus on delving into the deepest meanings of particular sayings of Jesus, or another holy text. Some Christian traditions use prayer beads and Catholics use a rosary.

Rowan Williams, the former Archbishop of Canterbury, is a relatively recent convert. He practises walking meditation – pacing very slowly and coordinating each step with an out-breath – as preparation for a period of silence or prayer. He has found that this awareness of his body in the present moment allows space for God to 'happen' in his life. 'The mature practitioner [not me] will discover . . . in "advanced" states, an awareness of unbroken inner light, with the strong sense of an action going on within that is quite independent of your individual will . . . a connection between God transcendent and God present and within.'[105]

Perhaps the most common approach to meditation is the silent repetition of a holy sound or mantra, which may have three or more separate sounds within it. Concentration on an object, which could be a statue or portrait, is another method. *Asana* yoga is the repeated practice and ultimate perfection of certain physical postures. Other forms of meditation include breath control or *pranayama*, focusing on an object or text, and immersing ourselves in complete silence.

The practice of meditation, depending upon the seriousness of the application and the state of the practitioner, takes us into the deepest realms. We gradually 'fall awake' as we become far more aware of our physical environment, the

---

[105] Williams, R. (2004). The Physicality of Prayer. *New Statesman*. July, 4–10, 2004.

people around us and the needs of the moment. We find ourselves becoming progressively less self-centred and more connected with others. We become calmer and happier. In time, and when we least expect it, we will experience levels of joy that surpass all our previous understanding of what we can experience.

In meditation, we do not have to acquire anything. We merely have to learn how to let go. Letting go of thoughts. Letting go of feelings. Letting go of our self-centred way of living. What is stopping us letting go, and practising meditation fully?

Make a note now of blockages you have to practising meditation, and to letting go of your attachment to your thoughts and feelings, possessions and even people around you. Why is your ego preventing you practising? Is it because it senses its own extinction? As long as we remain bonded and attached, we will never be free. Until we are free, we will never be fully alive. Until we are fully alive, we will never know joy.

Blockages to practising meditation
1
2
3
4
5

Contemplation

The word contemplation is derived from the Latin word *contemplari*, which probably originatated in the language of augury meaning to view attentively or to 'contemplate'.

Contemplation was seen by Plato as a way of allowing the soul to understand divine forms. Christianity stressed contemplation as a practice that allows us to have a vision of God, and to understand God in our own hearts and minds. Contemplation is the purposeful direction of the mind towards sacred texts and more broadly, the divine. It requires us to carve time out from our busy lives and to devote ourselves towards a pursuit of profundity and God. In Eastern Christianity, contemplation means seeing God.

Human beings have always been liable to get distracted from the present moment. In the earliest days it was fear of attack from animals or other humans. In our times it might be the lure of electronic media constantly entering our consciousness. We will never overcome our tendency to distraction without conscious efforts at mental and spiritual discipline.

St Ignatius Loyola (1491–1556), the founder of the Jesuits, suggested a daily exercise called 'The Examen'.[106] It consists of the following five elements:

- Recall you are in the presence of God.
- Look at your day with gratitude.

---

[106] Zagano, P. (2003). Examen of Consciousness: Finding God in All Things. *Catholic Update.*

- Ask help from the Holy Spirit.
- Review your day (including asking when you failed, and when you loved).
- Reconcile and resolve.

To contemplate properly we need to find not only time but also space, completely removed from worldly preoccupations. It requires devotion and profound application. Contemplation is not for the scatterbrained or for those who are not completely serious about wanting to understand truth at the deepest levels.

The person who successfully practises mindfulness, meditation or contemplation over a sustained period will acquire a personal knowledge and understanding that no one can ever take away. We live in the world only partially, because we are only partially here. We drive cars from one end of the city to another without being present. We can get through a whole day or week, month or year without ever being fully awake. Mindfulness, meditation and contemplation are processes of fully waking up. They are not about belief: they are about direct experience and knowledge.

As Anthony de Mello (1931–1987), the Indian Jesuit priest wrote, 'Spirituality means waking up. Most people, even though they don't know it, are asleep. They're born asleep, they live asleep, they marry in their sleep, they breed children in their sleep, they die in their sleep without ever waking up. They never understand the loveliness and the beauty of this thing that we call human existence.'[107]

---

[107] de Mello, A. (n.d.). *Spirituality means waking up*. Retrieved 3 October 2014

We can all wake up to what is real. We can only start to do so if we begin now.

We come from stillness and we return to stillness. Our journey in life is from silence to silence. A life well lived returns us to that point of infinite quiet from which we sprang.

We cast ourselves off into the great unknown. We abandon certainty. By bidding farewell to our partial possessions, we gain all possessions. By letting go of our life, we find life.

Iris Murdoch, the novelist and philosopher, argued for a mindful, present-moment approach to life in her late work, *The Sovereignty of Good* (1970). Drawing on the work of French mystical philosopher Simone Weil, she invites us to focus our attention on what is 'good', because doing so will connect us to the 'true nature of things'. She says attending to the present is 'the ultimate condition to be aimed at'. Doing so will make us 'humble': such a person 'sees himself as nothing' and can 'see other things as they are'.[108]

Meditation and mindfulness have allowed me to see at last Joanna as she is. Riven though her body is with cancer, I have never known her more beautiful and serene. Stripped of all thoughts, I see her before me, the thing itself, and I am filled by nothing but total love for her and the universe.

---

from http://demellospirituality.com/awareness/37.html.
[108] Quoted in Seldon, A. (2009). Trust. Biteback.

Conclusion

Thank you for joining me for the journey of this book. I have learnt much from writing it. It has caused me to reflect deeply on my own learning and mistakes in life. The suggested books that follow are deliberately few in number, but have all enriched my own life as I hope they might yours.

How far has reading this book, filling in and responding to the questions, taken you along the journey to greater happiness and joy? A teacher once told me that the more you put in, the more you get out, and I think that will be true of the exercises. You may find that returning to them in six months or a year will yield further thoughts and reflection, but for now, make a note of what you have learnt from doing the work, and what you might change in your life.

I still do not know what my ultimate purpose in life is. I can see that I have had a role as a teacher, as an explainer and as an unsettler of the status quo. As I leave one career, I am searching for the right move. I have a strong sense that my life to date has been a preparation for what is to come.

What I have learnt	What I will change in my life

At times the journey has been far from easy but I feel lighter now than at any point in my life before. Moving into the unknown fills me with intense excitement and anticipation. I hope you share this feeling as you come to the end of the book.

Bibliography

Further Reading

Culliford, L. (2011). *The Psychology of Spirituality: An Introduction.* Jessica Kingsley Publishers.

Eliot, T.S. (1979). *Four Quartets (1944).* London and Boston: Faber and Faber.

Gibran, K. (2012). *The Prophet: A New Annotated Edition.* Oneworld Publications.

Gollancz, V. (Ed.). (1956). *From Darkness to Light: A Confession of Faith in the Form of an Anthology.* Harper.

Graham, L. (2013). *Bouncing Back: Rewiring Your Brain for Maximum Resilience and Well-being.* New World Library.

Israel, M. (1974). *Summons to Life: The Search for Identity Through the Spiritual.* Hodder and Stoughton.

Kabat-Zinn, J. (2011). *Mindfulness for Beginners: Reclaiming the Present Moment—And Your Life.* Sounds True.

Rohr, R. (2011). *Falling Upward: A Spirituality for the Two Halves of Life.* John Wiley & Sons.

Schoch, R. (2006). *The Secrets of Happiness: Three Thousand Years of Searching for the Good Life.* Simon and Schuster.

Walker, S.P. (2010). *The Undefended Leader.* Piquant Editions.

Walsh, J. (Ed.). (1981). *The Cloud of Unknowing.* Paulist Press.

Also by Anthony Seldon

Churchill's Indian Summer (1981)

By Word of Mouth (with Joanna Pappworth, 1983)

Contemporary History (ed., 1987)

Ruling Performance (ed., with Peter Hennessy, 1987)

Political Parties Since 1945 (ed., 1988)

The Thatcher Effect (ed., with Dennis Kavanagh, 1989)

Politics UK (joint author, 1991)

Conservative Century (ed., 1994)

The Major Effect (ed., with Dennis Kavanagh, 1994)

The Heath Government 1970-1974
(ed., with Stuart Ball, 1996)

The Contemporary History Handbook
(ed., with Brian Brivati, etc, 1996)

The Ideas That Shaped Post-war Britain
(ed., with David Marquand, 1996)

How Tory Governments Fall (ed., 1996)

Major: A Political Life (1997)

10 Downing Street: An Illustrated History (1999)

The Powers Behind the Prime Minister
(with Dennis Kavanagh, 1999)

Britain Under Thatcher (with Daniel Collings, 2000)

The Foreign Office: An Illustrated History (2000)

The Blair Effect 1997–2001 (ed., 2001)

A New Conservative Century? (with Peter Snowdon, 2001)

Public and Private Education: The Divide Must End (2001)

Partnership not Paternalism (2002)

Brave New City (2002)

New Labour, Old Labour (ed., with Kevin Hickson, 2004)

Blair (2004)

The Conservative Party: An Illustrated History
(with Peter Snowdon, 2004)

The Blair Effect 2001–5 (ed., with Dennis Kavanagh, 2005)

Blair Unbound (2007)

Blair's Britain (ed. 2007)

An End to Factory Schools (2009)

Trust: How We Lost it and How We Get it Back (2009)

Brown at 10 (with Guy Lodge, 2010)

Why Schools? Why Universities? (2010)

The Politics of Optimism (2011)

Public Schools and the Great War (with David Walsh, 2013)

Schools United (2014)

The Architecture of Diplomacy: The British Embassy in Washington
(with Daniel Collings, 2014)

The Coalition Effect (ed., with Mike Finn, 2015)

Downing Street: An Illustrated History (2015)

Cameron at 10 (with Peter Snowdon, 2015)

Index

books to help you live a good life

Join the conversation and tell us how you live a #goodlife

🐦 @yellowkitebooks
📘 YellowKiteBooks
📌 Yellow Kite Books
📷 YellowKiteBooks